PSYCHOLOGY OF MOTIVATION

ARVIND UPADHYAY

Made with ♥ on the Notion Press Platform
www.notionpress.com

Most people we run into do what doesn't work, because most people try to motivate others by downloading their own anxiety onto them. Parents do this constantly; so do managers and leaders in the workplace. They get anxious about their people's poor performance, and then they download that anxiety onto their people. Now everybody's tense and anxious! Downloading your anxiety onto other people only motivates them to get away from you as quickly as possible. It doesn't motivate them to do what you really want them to do. It doesn't help them get the best out of themselves.Managers blame their own people for poor numbers, when it's really the manager's responsibility. CEOs blame their managers, when it's really the CEO. They call consultants in a panic, talk about the numbers, and then ask, "Do you recommend we implement FISH?" "FISH" is a current training fad that has a great deal of value in inspiring employees and focusing on the customer. But we don't deliver FISH in this book. We deliver an observation about fish. "A fish rots from the head down," we remind the manager whose people are not performing. And that's our version of FISH. So, the first step in motivating others is for you, if you're the leader wanting the motivation, to realize that "if there's a problem, I'm the problem." Once you truly get that, then you can use these 100 ways. The mastery of a few key paradoxes is vital. They are the paradoxes that have allowed our coaching and consulting to break through the mediocrity and inspire success where there was no success before. Paradoxes such as: 1. To get more done, slow down. 2. To get your point across, stop talking. 3. To hit your numbers faster, take them less seriously and make a game of it. 4. To really lead people, go ahead of them. These are a few of the paradoxes that open leadership up into a spiral of success you have never imagined.

We wanted to add in the best motivational tool of all: inspiration. How you can inspire your people by letting them watch you grow. Letting them see a "before" and "after" picture of you as you master more and more skills of excellent leadership.

Contents

Contents

Contents

1

WHERE MOTIVATION COMES

Leadership is the art of getting someone else to do something you want done because he wants to do it. —Dwight D. Eisenhower

There was a manager who came early to a seminar we were presenting on leadership. He was attired in an olive green polo shirt and white pleated slacks, ready for a day of golf. He walked to the front of the room and said, “Look, your session is not mandatory, so I’m not planning on attending.” “That’s fine, but I wonder why you came early to this session to tell us that. There must be something that you’d like to know.” “Well, yes, there is,” the manager confessed. “All I want to know is how to get my people on the sales team to improve. How do I manage them?” “Is that all you want to know?” “Yes, that’s it,” declared the manager. “Well, we can save you a lot of time and make sure that you get to your golf game on time.” The manager leaned forward, waiting for the words of wisdom that he could extract about how to manage his people. And we told him: “You can’t.” “What?”“You can’t manage anyone. So there, you can go and have a great game.” “What are you saying?” asked the manager. “I thought you give whole seminars on motivating others. What do you mean, I can’t?” “We do give whole seminars on this topic. But one of the first things we teach managers is that they can’t really directly control their people. Motivation always comes from within your employee, not from you.” “So what is it you do teach?” “We teach you how to get people to motivate themselves. That is the key. And you do that by managing agreements, not people. And that is what we are going to discuss this morning.” The manager put his car keys in his pocket and sat down in the first seat closest to the front of the room for the rest of the seminar. He has spent his whole life trying to manage the behavior and emotions of other people, at home as well as at work. Therefore, his life was full of stress and disappointment. We were going to show him that motivation comes from the inside, not the outside. 2. Teach Self-Discipline Discipline is remembering what you want. —David Campbell, Founder, Saks Fifth Avenue The myth that nearly everyone believes is that we "have" self-discipline. It's something in us, like a genetic gift, that we either have or we don't.

The truth is that we can all "have" self-discipline. The question is really whether or not we learn to develop and use self-discipline. Here's another way to realize it: Self-discipline is like a language. Any child can learn a language. (All children do learn a language, actually.) Any 90-year-old can also learn a new language. If you are 9 or 90 and you're lost in the rain in Juarez, it works when you use some Spanish to find your way to warmth and safety. It works. In this case, Spanish is like self-discipline in that you are using it for something. You were not born with the language, but you can learn it and use it. In fact, you can use as much or as little as you wish. And the more you use, the more you can make happen. If you were an American transferred to Juarez to live for a year and needed to make your living there, the more Spanish you spoke, the better it would be for you. If you had never spoken Spanish before, you could still use it like a tool. You could open your little English/Spanish phrases dictionary and start using it. You could ask for directions or help by using that little dictionary! You wouldn't need to have been born with any special language skills. The same is true with self-discipline, in the same exact way. Yet most people don't believe it. Most people think they either have it or they don't. Most people think it's a character trait or a permanent aspect of their personality. That's a profound mistake. That's a mistake that can ruin a life. But the good news is that it is never too late to correct that mistake in yourself and your people.

Listen to how people get this so wrong: "He would be my top salesperson if he had any selfdiscipline at all," a company leader recently said. "But he has none." Not true. He has as much self-discipline as anyone else does; he just hasn't chosen to use it yet. Just as we all have as many Spanish words to draw upon as anyone else. It is true that the more often I choose to go to my little dictionary and use the words, the easier it becomes to use Spanish. If I go enough times to the book, and practice enough words and phrases, it gets so easy to speak Spanish that it seems as if it's part of my nature, like it's something I "have" inside me. Just like golf looks as if it comes naturally to Tiger Woods. Self-discipline is the same. If the person you lead truly understood that self-discipline is something one uses, not something one has, then that person could use it to accomplish virtually any goal he or she ever set. That person could use it whenever he wanted, or leave it behind whenever he wanted. Instead, people worry. They worry about whether they've got what it takes. Whether it's "in" them. Whether their parents and guardians put it there. (Some think it's put there experientially; some think it's put there genetically. It's neither. It's never put "in" there at all. It's a tool that anyone can use. Like a hammer. Like a dictionary.) Enlightened leaders get more out of their people because they know that each of their people already has everything it takes to be successful. They don't buy the excuses, the apologies, and the sad fatalism that most nonperformers skillfully sell to their managers. They just don't buy in.

Don't tell people how to do things, tell them what to do and let them surprise you with their results. —George S. Patton You can't motivate someone who can't hear you. If what you're saying is bouncing off their psychological armor, it makes little difference how good you are at saying it. You are not being heard. Your people have to hear you to be moved by you. In order for someone to hear you, she must first be heard. It doesn't work the other way around. It doesn't work when you always go first because your employee must first appreciate that you are on her wavelength and understand her thinking completely. We were working with a financial services CEO named Lance who had difficulties with his four-woman major account team. They didn't care for him and didn't trust him, and they dreaded every meeting with him because he would go over their shortcomings. Lance was at his wit's end and asked for coaching. "Meet with each of them one at a time," we advised. "What do I say?" "Say nothing. Just listen." "Listen to what?" "The person across from you." "What's my agenda?" "No agenda."

"What do I ask them?" "How is life? How is life for you in this company? What would you change?" "Then what?" "Then just listen." "I don't know if I could do that." The source of his major account team's low morale had just been identified. The rest was up to Lance.

Shallow people believe in luck. Wise and strong people believe in cause and effect. —Ralph Waldo Emerson A masterful motivator of others asks, "What do we want to cause to happen today? What do we want to produce?" Those are the best management questions of all. People who have a hard time managing people simply have a hard time asking themselves those two questions, because they're always thinking about what's happening to them instead of what they're going to cause to happen. When your people see you as a cause instead of an effect, it won't be hard to teach them to think the same way. Soon, you will be causing them to play far beyond their own self-concepts. You can cause that to happen. But it all comes from who you are being from moment to moment. A producer or a critic?

We had the opportunity to watch and hear Neale Donald Walsch speak a couple years ago, and his message inspired us, as always. It's amazing who we can be if we are willing to drop the story of who we think we should be. In our coaching practice we have always marveled at the fact that people grow, evolve, and move forward the minute they are willing to live without their stories about themselves (weaknesses) and others (threats). Steve's book The Story of You came out of those breakthroughs in coaching sessions. Or, as Walsch has said, "Every decision you make— every decision—is not a decision about what to do. It's a decision about Who You Are. When you see this, when you understand it, everything changes. You begin to see life in a new way. All events, occurrences, and situations turn into opportunities to do what you came here to do." Choosing to be a producer who causes things to happen will set you apart from most other people. And that's not always easy. Most managers just try to manage like other people manage, and lose all the potential of who they could really be by doing that. Or, in the words of the fiery and brilliant philosopher Arthur Schopenhauer, "We forfeit three-fourths of ourselves to be like other people."

2

Distancing yourself from your own superiors.

Maybe you do this to win favor and create bonding at the victim level with the team, but it won't work. In fact, what you have done will eventually damage the confidence of the team. It will send three messages that are very damaging to morale and motivation: 1. This organization can't be trusted. 2. Our own management is against us. 3. Yours truly, your own team leader, is weak and powerless in the organization. This leads to an unpleasant but definite kind of bonding, but it also leads to deep trust problems and further disrespect for the integrity of the organization. Running down upper management can be done covertly (a rolling of the eyes at the mention of the CFO's name) or overtly ("I don't know why we're doing this, no one ever consults with me on company policy, probably because they know I'd disagree"). This mistake is deepened by the repeated use of the word "they." ("They want us to start...." "I don't know why they are having us do it this way...." "They don't understand what you guys are going through here...." "They, they, they....") The word they used in excess soon becomes a nearobscenity and solidifies the impression that we are isolated, misunderstood victims. A true leader has the courage to represent upper management, not run it down. A true leader never uses the word they to refer to senior officials in the company. A true leader says "we."

I can't motivate others if I am not doing the right thing. And to keep myself in a relaxed and centered state, it's important for me not to be scattered, distracted, or spread thin. It's important that I don't race around thinking that I've got too much to do, because I don't have too much to do. The truth is, there is only one thing to do, and that is the one thing

I have chosen to do right now. If I do that one thing as if it's all I have to think about, it will be extremely well done and my relationship with any other person involved in that task will be better and more relaxed and full of trust than before. A careful study of my past week shows me that I did a lot of things last week, and they all got done one thing at a time. In fact, even in my busiest time ever, I was only able to do one thing at a time, even though I stressed myself and other people out by always thinking of seven things at once so that when I talked to you all I could think about was the seven other people I needed to talk to. Sorry I seemed so disconnected to you when we talked. I apologize. And eventually all seven people felt that stress and that lack of attentiveness—that absolute lack of warmth. A person who thinks that he or she should try to do more than one thing at a time produces fear, adrenaline, and anxiety in the human system, and others pick up on that. That does not warm people, and they eventually want to keep away from it, so your relationships suffer. The mind entertains one thought at a time, and only one. Why fight it? The greatest cause of feeling "swamped" and "overwhelmed" in life is caused by not being willing to slow down and embrace that one thing the mind can think of. The greatest source of stress in the workplace is the mind's attempt to carry many thoughts, many tasks, many future scenarios, many cares, many worries, and many concerns at once. The mind can't do that. No mind can, not even Einstein's mind could. It can only carry one thing. Therefore, from now on, I want to choose ONE THING from the list of things that need to be done, and then do that one thing as if that were the only thing. If it's a phone call, then I need to slow down and relax and let myself be in a good, focused mood so that the phone call will be a complete experience, and the recipient and I can be upbeat afterward. Recently we talked to Jason, a national sales manager who had just finished a brutal, long phone conference with his team. He spent the conference call nervously urging on his team to higher numbers and warning them that the team goals were not going to be met at the rate they were going. He had called the meeting because his own superiors had just called him to question him about his team's poor performance. Although Jason had been working 12-hour days, he felt he was falling behind in everything. On top of that, his superiors' anxiety was then passed down to him. Because it was passed down into a hectic, disorganized mind, he freaked out and took it out on his team. This is not motivation. Motivation requires a calm, centered leader, focused on one thing, and only one thing. 7. Keep Giving Feedback The failure to give appropriate and timely feedback is the most extreme cruelty that we can inflict on any human being. —Charles Coonradt, Management Consultant Human beings crave feedback. Try ignoring any 3-year-old. At first, he will ask for positive attention, but if he is continually ignored, soon you will hear a loud crash or cry, because any feedback, even negative feedback, is better than no feedback. Some people think that this principle only applies to children. But it applies even more so to adults. The cruelest form of punishment in prison is solitary confinement. Most prisoners will do anything—even temporarily improve their behavior—to avoid being in a situation with little or no feedback. You may have heard of the relaxing effect of a sensory deprivation chamber. You are placed for a few minutes in a dark, cocoon-like chamber, floating in body-temperature salt water, with all light and sound cut off. It's great for a few minutes. But not for long.

3

Accelerate change

My role as a leader is always—always—to keep my people cheered up, optimistic, and ready to play full-out in the face of change. That's my job. Most managers do not see this as their job. They see their job as being babysitters, problem-solvers, and firefighters. And so they produce babies, problems, and fires all around them. In the face of change, this dysfunction is most painfully revealed. Therefore, it's important to anticipate the psychological reaction to change in your employees and to see how it follows a predictable cycle. Your employees pass through these four stages in the cycle, and you can learn how to manage this passage: The Change Cycle 1. Objection: "This can't be good." 2. Reduced Consciousness: "I really don't want to deal with this." 3. Exploration: "How can I make this change work for me?" 4. Buy-in: "I have figured out how I can make this work for me and for others." Sometimes the first three stages in the cycle take a long, long time for your people to pass through. Productivity and morale can take a dizzying dip as employees resist change. It is human nature to resist change. We all do it. We hate to get into the shower and then we hate to get out. But if I am a very good leader, I'll want to thoroughly understand the change cycle so that I can get my people to stage 4—the "Buy-in"—as soon as humanly possible. I want their total and deep buy-in to make this change work for them, for me, and for the company. So how do I help move them through stages 1, 2, and 3? First of all, I prepare myself to communicate about this change in the most enthusiastic and positive way possible. And I mean prepare. As many great coaches have said, "It isn't the will to win that wins the game, it's the will to prepare to win." So I want to prepare myself. I want to educate and inform myself about the change so I can be an enthused spokesperson in favor of the change. Most managers don't do this. They realize that their people are resisting the change, so they identify with the loyal resistance. They sympathize with the outcry. They give voice to what a hassle the change is. They even apologize for it. They say it shouldn't have happened. "This never should have happened. I'm sorry. With all you go through already, it's a shame there's this now, too." A remark that cultivates victims! Every internal change is made to improve the viability or effectiveness of the company. That truth is the one I want to sell. I want my people to see what's in this for them. I want them to really see for themselves that a more viable company is a more secure place to work. What about change from the outside? Regulators, market shifts, vendor problems? In those cases I want to stress to my team that the competition faces the same changes. When it rains on the field, it rains on both teams. Then I want to stress the superiority of our team's rain strategy so that this rain becomes our advantage. I also want to keep change alive on my team as a positive habit. Yes, we change all the time. We look forward to change. We even have fun changing before we have to.

The people you motivate will tend to divide themselves into two categories: owners and victims. This distinction comes from Steve's Reinventing Yourself, Revised Edition (Career Press, 2005), which reveals in detail how owners are people who take full responsibility for their happiness, and victims are always lost in their unfortunate stories. Victims blame others, victims blame circumstance, and victims are hard to deal with. Owners own their own morale. They own their response to any situation. (Victims blame the situation.) At a recent seminar, a company CEO named Marcus approached Steve at the break: "I have a lot of victims working for me," Marcus said. "It's a part of our American culture today," Steve answered.

"Yeah, I know, but how can I get them to recognize their victim tendencies?" "Try something else instead," Steve said. "Try getting excited when they are not victims. Try pointing out their ownership actions; try acknowledging them when they are proactive and self-responsible." "Okay. What are the best techniques to use with each type of person?" Marcus asked. "I mean, I have both. I have owners, too. Do you treat them differently?" "With the owners in your life, you don't need techniques. Just appreciate them," Steve said. "And you will. With the victims, be patient. Hear their feelings out empathetically. You can empathize with their feelings without buying in to their victim's viewpoint. Show them the other view. Live it for them. They will see with their own eyes that it gets better results." "Can't I just have you come in to give them a seminar in ownership?" Marcus asked. "In the end, even if we were to train your staff in ownership thinking, you would still have to lead them there every day, or it would be easy to lose. Figure your own ways to lead them there. Design ways that incorporate your own personality and style into it. There is no magic prescription. There is only commitment. People who are committed to having a team of self-responsible, creative, upbeat people will get exactly that. Leaders whose commitment isn't there won't get it. The three basic things you can do are: (1) Reward ownership wherever you see it. (2) Be an owner yourself. (3) Take full responsibility for your staff's morale and performance." Marcus looked concerned. We could tell he still wasn't buying everything.

"What's troubling you?" Steve asked. "Don't be offended." "Of course not." "How do I turn around a victim without me appearing to be that annoying 'positive thinker'?" "You don't have to come off as an annoying positive thinker to be a true leader. Just be realistic, honest, and upbeat. Focus on opportunities and possibilities. Focus on the true and realistic upside. Don't gossip or run down other people. There is no reliable trick that always works, but in our experience, when you are a really strong example of ownership, and you clearly acknowledge it and reward it and notice it in other people (especially in meetings, where victims can hear you doing it), it gets harder and harder for people to play victim in that setting. Remember that being a victim is essentially a racket. It is a manipulation. You don't have to pretend that it's a valid point of view intellectually, because it is not." "Okay, I see. That sounds doable," Marcus said. "But there's one new employee I'm thinking about. He started out great for a few months, but now he seems so lost and feels betrayed. That's his demeanor, anyway. How do I instill a sense of ownership in him?" "You really can't 'instill' it," said Steve. "Not directly. Ownership, by its nature, is grown by the owner of the ownership. But you can encourage it, and nourish it when you see it. You can nurture it and reward it. You can even celebrate it. If you do all those things, it will appear. Like a flower in your garden. You don't make the flower grow, but if you do certain things, it will appear."

4

lead from front

There is nothing more motivational than leading from the front. It motivates others when you are out there and you do it yourself. It's inspiring to them when you do what you want them to do. Be inspiring. Your people would rather be inspired than fixed or corrected. They would rather be inspired than anything else. As a motivational practice, leading from the front hits harder and lasts longer than any other practice. It changes people more deeply and more completely than anything else you can do. So be what you want to see. If you want your people to be more positive, be more positive. If you want them to take more pride in their work, take more pride in yours. Show them how it's done. If you want them to look good and dress professionally, look better yourself. Want them to be on time? Always be early (and tell them why...tell them what punctuality means to you, not to them). And as General George Patton (a soul mate of Gandhi's) said, "There are three principles of leadership: (1) Example, (2) Example, and (3) Example."

5

Role of thought

Business and life coach JacQuaeline told us this story about a mechanic in a school district complaining of punching a time clock and doing the same thing on his job over and over for the last 20 years. "I'm burned out and need a change!" the mechanic declared. "Possibly," JacQuaeline replied. "But you might want to try learning to love what you are resisting, because if you don't, you will likely run into it in your next job too, in another guise." The mechanic responded, "I can love what I'm resisting? I'm not sure that I believe that's possible, but even if I did, how is it done?" "Well," his coach said, "what is a higher purpose to your job than just turning nuts and bolts every day?" "That's easy," replied the mechanic. "The higher purpose of my job is saving children's lives every day." "Yes, that's great!" whispered the coach. "Now, every morning when you get into your higher purpose, saving children's lives every day, you will be clear that your job and responsibility is so important that the time clock almost won't matter anymore."

She had given him a new way to think. She had put him in touch with the power of higher thought to transform experience. Make certain all the people you want to motivate understand the role of thought in life. There is nothing more important. A: I'm depressed. B: You just think you're depressed. A: Same thing...it feels like the same thing. B: It feels like the same thing, because it is the same thing. A: What if I thought I was really happy? B: I think that would make you feel really happy. A: I know it would. Why is it that the rain depresses one person and makes another person happy? If things "make you" feel something, why does this thing called rain make one person feel one thing and the other person feel the other thing? Why, if things make you feel something, doesn't the rain make both people feel the same thing? One person you lead might say, "Oh no, bad weather, how depressing." Another person might say, "Oh boy, we have some wonderful, refreshing rain!" Because the rain doesn't actually make you feel anything. (No person, place, or thing can make you feel anything.) It is the thought about the rain that causes your feeling. And throughout all your leadership adventures, you can teach your people this most important concept: the causal power of thought.

One person thinks (just thinks!) the new pay plan is great. The other person thinks (but just thinks) the plan is depressing. Nothing in the world has any meaning until they give it meaning. Nothing in the workplace does either. Your people often look to you for meaning. What does this new directive really mean? Do you sense the opportunity you have? We can make things mean anything we want them to, within reason. Why not use that power? People don't make your employees angry; their own thoughts make them angry. They can't be angry unless they think the thoughts that make them angry. If your nastiest employee wins the lottery in the morning, who's going to make her angry that day? No one. No matter what anyone says to her, she isn't going to care. She's not going to give it another thought. Your employees can only get angry with someone if they think about that person as a threat to their happiness. If they don't think about that, how can they be angry? Your people are free to think about anything they want. They have absolute freedom of thought. The highest IQ ever measured in any human being was achieved by Marilyn vos Savant, many years in a row. Someone once asked Marilyn what the relationship was between feeling and thinking. She said, "Feeling is what you get for thinking the way you do." People feel motivated only when they think motivated thoughts. Thought rules. Circumstance does not rule. The closer your relationship to that truth, the better the leader you are.

6
Tell the truth quickly

Question: How many legs does a dog have if you call the tail a leg? Answer: Four. Calling a tail a leg doesn't make it a leg. —Abraham Lincoln Great leaders always share a common habit: they tell the truth faster than other managers do. Steve recalls his work with helping managers motivate salespeople. (And notice that this doesn't just apply to salespeople. It applies to all people.) I always found that people would tell me about their limitations, and I would listen patiently and try to talk them out of their limitations, and they would try to talk me back into what their limitations really were. Limitation seemed to be their fixation. One day, I was working with a salesperson in a difficult one-on-one coaching session, and finally I just blurted it out (I guess I was tired, or upset, or was having a stressful day), and I said, "You know, you're just lying to me." "What?" he said. "You're lying. Don't tell me there's nothing you can do. There's a lot you can do. So let's you and I work with the truth, because if we work with the truth and we don't lie to each other, we are going to get to your success so much faster than if we do it this way, focusing on your self-deceptions." Well, my client was just absolutely shocked. He stared at me for a long time. It's not always a great relationshipbuilder to call someone a liar. I don't recommend it. If I hadn't been as tired as I was, I don't think I would have done it, but the remarkable thing was, my client all of a sudden began to smile! He sat back in his chair and he said, "You know what? You are right." I said, "Really?" He said, "You are right, that's not the truth at all, is it?" "No, it's not." "You are right," he said. "There's a lot I can do." "Yes, there is." This is the main lie you hear in the world of business and especially in sales: "There's nothing I can do." This is the "I am helpless and powerless" lie. The truth is, there is always a lot you can do. You just have to choose the most creative and efficient way to do it. As Shakespeare wrote, "Action is eloquence." One way a salesperson we know starts her day with action is to ask herself, "If I were coaching me, what would I advise myself to do right now? What creative action would bring the highest return to me?" Another quick cure for the feeling that "there's nothing I can do" is to ask ourselves, "If I were my customer or my prospect, what would I want me to do?" And what you can always do is GIVE. Great salespeople, and any people who lead their teams in performance and who prosper the most from their profession, are great givers. They stay in constant touch with their power to do so much by constantly giving their internal and external clients beneficial things—helpful information, offers of service, respect for their time, support for their success, cheerful friendly encounters, sincere acknowledgments, the inside scoop—giving, giving, giving all day long, always putting the client's wants and needs first. They always ask the best questions and always listen better than anyone else listens. As that commitment grows and expands, and those gifts of attention are lavished on each client in creative and ongoing communications, that salesperson becomes a world-level expert in client psychology and buying behavior. And that salesperson also realizes that such a dizzying level of expertise can only be acquired through massive benefit-based interaction! A new week begins, and this thought occurs: "There's so much good I can do, I just can't wait."

7

Don't confuse stressing out

Stress, in addition to being itself and the result of itself, is also the cause of itself. —Hans Selye, Psychologist Most managers try double negatives as a way to motivate others. First, they intentionally upset themselves over the prospect of not reaching their goals, and then they use the upset as negative energy to fire up the team. It doesn't work. Stressing out over our team's goals is not the same as caring about them. Stressing out is not a useful form of motivation. No performer, when tense, or stressed, performs well. No leader does. No salesperson. No athlete. No fund-raiser. No field-goal kicker. No free-throw shooter. No parent. A stressed-out, tense performer only has access to a small percent of his brain. If your favorite team is playing, / 45 do you want a tense, stressed-out person shooting a free throw, or kicking a long field goal in the last moments of the game? Or would you rather see a confident, calm player step up to the challenge? Most people stress themselves out as a form (or a show) of "really caring" about hitting some goal. But it's not caring, it's stressing out. Stressing out makes one perform worse. True caring makes one perform better. That's why it's vital for a leader to know the difference. The two couldn't be more different. Caring is relaxing, focusing, and calling on all of your resources, all of that relaxed magic, all of that lazy dynamite you bring to bear when you pay full attention with peace of mind. No one performs better than when he or she is relaxed and focused. "Stress is basically a disconnection from the Earth," says the great creativity teacher Natalie Goldberg. "It's a forgetting of the breath. Stress is an ignorant state. It believes that everything is an emergency." It is not necessary to stress that way. Leadership success comes from knowing to focus and remain focused. Anything you pay attention to will expand. So don't spend your attention any old place. Spend it where you want the greatest results: in clients, customers, money, whatever. In a relaxed and happy way, you can be undivided and peaceful and powerful. You can succeed.

8

manage your superiors

Jean was an administrator in a large hospital system with which we were working. She welcomed the coaching work we were doing but had a pressing question about her own leadership. “We have had a lot of different bosses to report to,” Jean said. “It seems that just when we’re used to working for a certain CEO, the hospital brings in someone new.” “What exactly is the problem with that?” we asked. “Well, with so many changes in leadership over the years,” Jean asked, “how do we develop trust in the process?” “By trusting the process. Trust is not the same as verification. Trust risks something. And it is not necessarily bad or good that leadership changes. The question is, can you teach yourself to live and work peacefully with the change? It’s not whether it has changed so much, but rather this: What are you going to do to capitalize on the change?” “What if we don’t like the leadership now?” she pressed on. “What don’t you like?” “We get mixed messages from them!” Jean said. “And how can you keep asking us to take ownership when we get mixed messages from senior management?” “Every large organization we have ever worked with has had to confront, in varying degrees, this issue of ‘mixed messages.’ Mixed messages happen because people are only human and it’s hard to coordinate a lot of energetic, creative people to present themselves as one narrow message.” “I agree,” said Jean. “But it’s a challenge.” “It’s a challenge that must be dealt with. But it is not necessary to use it as a source of defeat or depression. It’s / 47 a challenge. We have often seen the ‘message from the top’ become more coherent and unified when the request for unity ‘from below’ becomes more benevolent and creative.” “You’re saying I should manage them a little better,” Jean said. “Exactly.” “With the key words being ‘benevolent’ and ‘creative’?” “Those would be the key words.”

9

Put Your Hose Away

Why are so many managers ineffective leaders? Because they are firefighters. When you become a firefighter, you don't lead anymore. You don't decide where your team is going. The fire decides for you. (The fire is whatever current problem has flared up and captured your time and imagination.) The fire controls your life. You think you are controlling the fire, but the fire is controlling you. You become unconscious of opportunity. You become blind to possibilities, because you are engulfed in, and defined by, the fire. If you're an unmotivational manager, even when you put the fire out, you hop back on the truck and take off across the company looking for another fire. Soon, all you know is fires, and all you know how to do is fight them. Even when there is no real fire, you'll find something you'll redefine as a fire because you are a firefighter and always want to be working. A great motivator doesn't fight fires 24/7. A true motivator leads people from the present into the future. The only time a fire becomes relevant is when it's in the way of that future goal. Sometimes a leader doesn't even have to put the fire out. She sometimes just takes a path around (or above) the fire to get to the desired future. A firefighter, on the other hand, will stop everything and fight every fire. That's the basic difference between an unconscious manager (letting the fires dictate activity) and a conscious leader (letting desired goals dictate activity).

Here's a question often asked: Isn't leadership something people are born with? Aren't some people referred to as born leaders? Yes, but it's a myth. Leadership is a skill, like gardening or chess or playing a computer game. It can be taught and it can be learned at any age if the commitment to learn is present. Companies can turn their managers into leaders. But if companies could transform all their managers into leaders, why wouldn't every company just do that?

They don't know what a leader is. So how can they train for it? They don't read books on leadership, they don't have leadership training seminars, and they don't hold meetings in which leadership is discussed and brainstormed. Therefore, they can't define it. So they say people are born leaders. The remedy for this is to always revise your picture of what a good leader is. People are not motivated by people who can't even picture good leadership. In his powerful, innovative book on business management, The Laughing Warriors (Lumina Media, 2003), Dale Dauten offers a picture of a leader with a code to work by: "THINK LIKE A HERO (Who can I help today?), WORK LIKE AN ARTIST (What else can we try?), REFUSE TO BE ORDINARY (Pursue excellence, then kill it.), and CELEBRATE (But take no credit.)." Continuously picturing that code in and of itself would create leadership.

10

Manage agreement, Not People

"Does anybody here work with a person who seems unmanageable?" Steve asked as he opened one of his leadership seminars.The managers who filled the room nodded and smiled. Some rolled their eyes skyward in agreement. They obviously had a lot of experience trying to manage people like that. "How do you do it?" one manager called out. "How do you manage unmanageable people?" "I don't know," Steve said. "What do you mean you don't know? We're here to find out how to do it," someone else called out. "I've never seen it done," Steve said. "Because I believe, in the end, all people are pretty unmanageable. I've never known anyone who was good at managing people." "Then why have a seminar on managing people if it can't be done?" "Well, you tell me, can it be done? Do you actually manage your people? Do you manage your spouse? Can you do it? I don't think so." "Well, then, is class dismissed?" "No, certainly not. Because we can all stay and learn how great leaders get great results from their people. But maybe they do it without managing people, because basically you can't manage people." "If they don't manage people, what do they do?" "They manage agreements." Managers make a mistake when they try to manage their people. They end up trying to shovel mercury with a pitchfork, managing people's emotions and personalities. Then they try to "take care" of their most upset people, not in the name of better communication and understanding, but in the name of containing dissent and being liked. This leads to poor time management and a lot of ineffective amateur psychotherapy. It also encourages / 51 employees to take a more immature position in their communication with management, almost an attempt to be re-parented by a supervisor rather than having an adultto-adult relationship. A leader's first responsibility is to make sure the relationship is a mature one. A skillful leader does not run around playing amateur psychotherapist, trying to manage people's emotions and personalities all day. A skillful leader is compassionate, and always seeks to understand the feelings of others. But a skillful leader does not try to manage those feelings. A leader, instead, manages agreements. A leader creates agreements with team members and enters into those agreements on an adult-to-adult basis. All communication is done with respect. There is no giving in to the temptation to be intimidating, bossy, or all-knowing. Once agreements are made on an adult-to-adult basis, people don't have to be managed anymore. What gets managed is the agreement. It is more mature and respectful to do it that way, and both sides enjoy more open and trusting communication. There is also more accountability running both ways. It is now easier to discuss uncomfortable subjects. Harry was an employee who always showed up late for team meetings. Many managers would deal with this problem by talking behind Harry's back, or trying to intimidate Harry with sarcasm, or freezing Harry out by not returning his calls, or meeting with Harry to play therapist. But our client Jill would do none of that. Jill co-authored an agreement with Harry that said Harry (and Jill) would both be on time for meetings.

They agreed to agree, and they agreed to keep their commitment to the agreement. It is an adult process that leads to open communication and relaxed accountability. Jill has come to realize that when adults agree to keep their agreements with each other, it leads to a more openly accountable company culture. It leads to higher levels of self-responsibility and self-respect. The biggest beneficial impact of managing agreements is on communication. It frees communication up to be more honest, open, and complete. A commitment to managing agreements is basically a commitment to being two professional adults working together, as opposed to "I'm your dad, I'm your father, I'm your mother, I'm your parent, and I will re-parent you. You're a child, and you're bad and you've done wrong, and I'm upset with you, and I'm disappointed in you, and I know that you've got your reasons and you've got your alibis and your stories, but still, I'm disappointed in you." That kind of approach is not management, it's not leadership, it's not even professional. That kind of approach, which we would say eight out of 10 managers do, is just a knee-jerk, intuitively parent-child approach to managing human beings. The problem with parent-child management is that the person being managed does not feel respected in that exchange. And the most important, the most powerful, precondition to good performance is trust and respect. Let's say my project leader has been assigned to get the team to do something. The team all agreed to watch a video and then take a certain test about it given on the Internet. But then they don't do it! What does it mean / 53 that they won't do things like that? What does it mean about them? What does it mean about me? All it means is that the person in charge of getting that project done is someone with whom I need to strengthen my agreement. It's not someone who's done something "wrong." I don't need to call them on the carpet. It's someone with whom I don't have a very strong agreement. And so I need to sit down with him or get into a good phone conversation with him, and say, "You and I need an agreement on this because this is something that must be done, and I want to have it done in the way that you can do it the most effectively, that won't get in the way of your day-to-day work. So let's talk about this. Let me help you with this so that it does get done. It's not an option, so you and I must come up with a way together, that we can both co-author, together, an agreement on how this is going to get done." Then I should ask these questions of that person: "Are you willing to do this? Is this something you can make sure your people follow up on? Do you have a way of doing it? Do you need my support?" And finally, at the end of the conversation, I've got that person agreeing with me about the project. Now, notice that this agreement is two-sided. So I also, as the co-professional in this agreement, am agreeing to certain things, too. That person might have said, "You know, one of the hard things about this is we don't have anything to watch this video on, we don't have a TV monitor in the store." And so I would say, "If I can get you a TV for your store, will that be all you need?"

"Yes, it will." "Well, here's what you can count on: By Friday, I'll have a TV monitor in the store. What else can I do for you?" Because a leader is always serving, too. Not just laying down the law, but serving. And always asking, "How can I assist you? How can I serve you and help you with this?" Because the true leader wants an absolute promise and absolute performance. And now that we have agreed, I ask very sincerely, "Can I count on you now to have this done, with 100-percent compliance? Can I count on that from you?" "Yes, of course you can." Great. We shake. Two professionals are leaving this meeting with an agreement they both made out of mutual respect, out of professional, grown-up conversation. Nobody had to be "managed."

11

Focus on Result Rather Excuse

A leader has to be able to change an organization that is dreamless, soulless and visionless...someone's got to make a wake-up call. —Warren Bennis If you are a sales manager, you probably run into the same frustrations that Frank conveyed to us when we talked last week. "I believe I need advice on how to deliver the 'Just Do It' message to my people," Frank said. "I've said it every way I can, and I think I'm starting to sound like a broken record. I don't know why I called you. I thought maybe you were advising your clients to pick up some new book to read, or that you might have some general words of wisdom." "What, specifically, is your problem?" "Half of the people on the team I manage are total non-producers!" he said. "And I keep telling them...it's not magical...it's getting the leads...and getting it done.... I've said, 'Just get off your butt, and go get referrals, make 60 to 75 phone calls, visit with eight to 10 potential buyers each week and watch how successful you'll be.'" "What's really missing here?" we asked him. "What's wrong with your picture? Why aren't they out there doing what would lead to sales?" "That's why I called you. If I knew what was missing, I wouldn't have called you." "Because it isn't 'just doing it' that is missing from the non-producers' equation. Although we always think it is. What's really missing runs deeper than that. What's really missing is the 'just wanting it.'" "Oh, I know they all say they want it. They want the commissions and they want the success." "They don't want it, or they would have it." "Oh, so you think people get everything they want?" "Actually, yes they do." "Really? I don't see that." "That's what we humans are all about. We know how to get what we want. We are biological systems designed to do that." We talked longer. There was something we wanted Frank to see: Frank's non-producers are under-producing because they do not want to produce. Not deep down. If you are a manager you must understand that. If you are a non-producer, you must understand that. Non-producers are simply not focusing all their attention on succeeding at selling. If they were, they would be producers. Even if they say they are focused on results, they're not. They are in sales because of other reasons...they believe they need the money, maybe, and therefore think they "should be" there. But they can't get any intellectual or motivational leverage from "should." "Should" sets them up for failure because it implies that they are still a child, and that they are trying to live up to other people's expectations—the expectation of the spouse, family, or society. But there's no power in that. No focus. No leverage. Salespeople who do what they think they "should do" all day convert their managers into parents. Then they ageregress into childhood and whine and complain. Even when you try to micromanage their activities, even when you are eloquent in showing them that Activity A leads to Result B (always) and Result B leads to Result C (always), they still do it halfheartedly and search in vain for a new "how to" from other mentors and peers. Frank now begins to see this form of dysfunction quite clearly, but he still doesn't know what to do about it. What Frank needs to manage is the want to, not the how to. Frank needs a quick course in outcome-management because, like most people, he is stuck in the world of processmanagement. The real joy of leadership can only come when you're getting results.

"Tell me what I, as a manager, ought to do," he said, after he realized that he already understood this whole idea. "Once you get the non-producer's sales goal (plan, quota, numbers) in front of you for mutual discussion," we said, "you need to draw out and cultivate the 'why.' Ask the person, 'Why do you want this? What will it do for you? What else will it do for you? What's one thing more it will do for you? If I were to tell you that there were activities that would absolutely get you to this number, would you do these activities? If not, why not? Would you promise both yourself and me that you would do these activities until you hit the number? Why not?'" If you're a manager like Frank, please keep in mind that you have people who don't really want what they are telling you they want, and even they don't realize that. You know that if they truly wanted to be producers, nothing in the world could stop them. "Intention Deficit Disorder" is what we have named the dysfunction that is always at the core of non-production. It is not a deficit in technique or know-how. Technique and know-how are hungrily acquired by the person who has an absolute and focused intention to succeed. The real long-term trick to good management is to hire people who want success. Once you have mastered that tricky art form, you will always succeed. But we get lazy in the hiring process and look for and listen for all the wrong things. Why do we do this? Why do we miss this crucial lack of desire in the hiring process? This is why: the person we hire really has a big "want to"—but only when it comes to getting the job. They really want the job. However, this is distinctly different than wanting to succeed at the job. These are two completely different goals. So we are hazy in the interviewing process, only half-listening, and we mistake the burning desire to get the job with a burning desire to succeed. It is a completely different and separate thing. The best managers we have ever trained always took more time and trouble in the hiring process than any of their competitors did. Then, once they had hired ambitious people, they based their management on the management of those people's personal goals. When sales managers learned to link the activity of cold-calling to the salesperson's most specific personal goals, cold-calling became something much more meaningful. These managers were spending their days managing results, not activities. Their positive reinforcement was always for results, not for activities.

12

try the outcome

Unless commitment is made, there are only promises and hopes...but no plans. —Peter F. Drucker Every non-producer you are managing is in some form of conflict. They say they want to succeed and hit their numbers, but their activities say otherwise. They themselves can't even see it, but you, the manager, can, and it drives you nuts. Finally, you have that talk that you always have, wherein you say to them, "I have a feeling that I want this for you more than you want it for yourself."And they get misty-eyed and their tears well up while they insist you are wrong. And you, being such a compassionate person, believe them! So you give them yet another chance to prove it to you. You do all kinds of heroics for them and waste all your time on them when your time could be better spent with your producers. Always remember that the time you spend helping a producer helps your team's production more than the time you spend with your non-producer. Some research we have seen shows that managers spend more than 70 percent of their time trying to get non-producers to produce. And most producers, when they quit for another job, quit because they didn't get enough attention. They didn't feel as if the company appreciated them enough nor could they grow fast enough in their position. If you help a producer who is selling 10 muffins a week learn how to sell 15, you have moved them up to 150 percent of their former level, and, even better, you have added five muffins to your team's total. If you were to spend that time, instead, with a non-producer, and get them up to 150 percent, you might have just moved them up from two muffins to three. You've only added one muffin (instead of five) to the team total. Most managers spend most of their days with the non-producer...adding one muffin to the team's total. Managers need to simplify, simplify, simplify. They do not need to do what they normally do: complicate, multitask, and complicate. Keep it as simple as you can for your non-producers, focusing on outcomes and results only. Spend more and more time with producers who are looking for that extra edge you can give them.

Non-producers have a huge lesson to learn from you. They could be learning every day that their production is a direct result of their own desire (or lack of it) to hit that precise number. People figure out ways to get what they want. Most non-producers want to keep their jobs (because of their spousal disapproval if they lose it, because of their fear of personal shame if they lose it, and so on), so all their activity is directed at keeping the job from one month to the next. If they can do the minimum in sales and still keep their job, they are getting what they want. People get what they want. The manager's challenge is to redirect all daily effort toward hitting a precise number. If your people believed that they had to hit that number, they would hit that number, and technique would never be an issue. Skills would never be an issue. They would find them. They would try out every technique in the book until that number appeared. Somehow, non-producers have convinced themselves that there is no direct cause and effect between increasing certain activities and hitting their numbers. Do you remember those little toy robots or cars you had when you were a kid that would bump into a wall and then turn 30 degrees and go again? If you put one of those toys in a room with an open door, it will always find the way out the door. Always. It is programmed to do so. It is mechanically programmed to keep trying things until it is out of there. That's also what top producers program themselves to do. It's the same thing. They keep trying stuff until they find a way. If they bump into a wall, they immediately turn 30 degrees and set out again.

people are trying, he has broken the cause-and-effect link. If you, as manager, ask them, "How much X do you do?" they will ask, "How do I learn a better technique for X?" And while better techniques are always good, it's not the point here. You are now discussing results. They will subconsciously try to steer you away from results into technique. Just like a child does with a parent! "Dad, I tried, but I can't! I can't do it!" Discuss technique after the commitment to results is clarified. Non-producers, at the deepest level, do not yet want to get the result. You have to understand this so you won't go crazy trying to figure them out. They don't want the result. They want the job. They want your approval. They want to be seen as "really trying." But deep down, they don't want the result. It's that simple. The truly great managers spend most of their time helping good producers go from 10 muffins to 15. They have fun. They are creative. They feed off of their producers' skills and enthusiasm. Their teams constantly outperform other teams. Why? Because other teams' managers have been hypnotized by their non-producers. Their nonproducers actually become good salespeople selling the wrong thing. Selling you the worst thing: "there is no cause and effect...there is no guarantee." Simplify. Focus on results. You will always get what you focus on. If you merely focus on activities, that's what you'll get: a whole lot of activities. But if you focus on results, that's what you'll get: a whole lot of results.

13

Create a game

Although some people think that life is a battle, it is actually a game of giving and receiving. —Florence Scovel Shinn, Philosopher/Author Complete this sentence with the first word that pops into your head: "Life is a ____." What came to mind first? (Let's hope the popular bumper sticker, "Life is a Bitch and Then You Die" did not come to mind.) Whatever comes to mind first, here's something that you (and we) can be sure of: that is exactly how life now is for you. What was your answer? In a poll of mid-level managers, the most common answer was "Life is a battle." But in a poll of senior executives, the most common answer was "Life is a game." Which version of life would you choose if you had a choice? To be as motivational a leader as you can possibly be, you might want to show your people that life with you is a game. What makes any activity a game? There needs to be some way to keep score, to tell whether people are winning or losing. Then it becomes pure fun. So be clear that although all kinds of prizes may be attached to the game, the game itself is being played for the sheer fun of it. How can you incorporate this into your life?

Chuck Coonradt, a longtime friend and mentor, is a management consultant and the best-selling author of The Game of Work. He has created an entire system for making a game out of work. Chuck recalled that when he started in the grocery business, in the icy frozen-food section of the warehouse, he noticed that the owners would bend over backwards to take care of their workers. They would give them breaks every hour to warm up and they would give them preferential pay. But no matter what they did, the workers would bitterly complain about the chilling cold. "However, you could take these exact same workers and put a deer rifle into their hands," Chuck said, "and you could send them out into weather that was much worse than anything in the warehouse, and they would call it fun! And you wouldn't have to pay them a dime! In fact, they would pay for it themselves!" The key to making work fun, as Tom Sawyer taught us many years ago, is to turn what most people would consider drudgery into a game. Randy was a leader-client of ours who had a problem with absenteeism. For many months he tried to attack and eliminate the problem. Finally, he realized that it might be possible to lighten things up by introducing the game element. So Randy created a game. (Leaders create; managers react.) He issued a playing card to every employee who achieved perfect attendance for the month. A card was drawn at random from a bucket of cards. The employee then put the card up in his or her cubicle. At the end of six months, the person with the best poker hand won a major prize; the second and third best hands also won good cash prizes.

"My absenteeism problem virtually disappeared," Randy later recalled. "In fact, we had some problems with actual sick people trying to work when they shouldn't have. They would wake up with a fever, and their spouse would say, 'You're staying home today,' and they would say, 'Are you crazy? I'm holding two aces and you want me to stay home?'" After being in business for four years selling a prepackaged management development program, Chuck Coonradt made what became the most important sales call of his career. He called on a plant manager in a pre-constructed housing company. As part of their discussion, the manager began to give Chuck the "Kids Today" lecture—kids don't care, kids won't work, kids don't have the same values you and I had when we were growing up. "As he was speaking, we were looking over the factory floor from the management office 30 feet above the factory floor," Chuck recalled. "He pointed down to the eight young men siding a house and said, 'What are you and your program going to do about that?'" Chuck said that he looked at their work pace and said that it "would best be compared to arthritic snails in wet cement. These guys appeared to be two degrees out of reverse and leaning backwards! He had given me objections for which I didn't have an answer. I really didn't know what to say." Then an amazing thing occurred—lunch. As soon as the lunch bell rang, these eight workers dropped their hammers as if they were electrified, took off on a dead run as if being stuck with cattle prods, four of them taking off their shirts, running 50 yards down the factory floor to a basketball court.

The motivational transformation was amazing! Chuck watched the game, mesmerized, for exactly 22 minutes. Everybody knew their job on the court, did their job on the court, and supported the team with energy, engagement, and enthusiasm—all without management. They knew how to contribute to the teams they were on, and they enjoyed it. At 12:22 the game stopped, they picked up their sack lunches and their sodas, and began to walk back to their workstations, where, at 1 p.m., they were back on the clock—arthritic snails back in the wet cement. Chuck turned to the plant manager and said, "I don't believe there is a raw human material problem. I don't think there is anything wrong with these kids' motivation." And on that day, Chuck began a quest to see if it would be possible to transfer the energy, enthusiasm, and engagement that he saw on the basketball court to the factory work floor. His success at doing so has become legendary throughout the business world. "Now we identify the motivation of recreation and bring it to the workplace," Chuck says. "The motivation of recreation includes feedback, scorekeeping, goal-setting, consistent coaching, and personal choice."

14

know your purpose

It is hard to motivate others if you don't have time to talk to them. There are fewer discouraging sights than a human chicken running around with his head cut off— and not enough time to find it. Managers whose teams are not performing up to expectations are simply doing ineffective things all day. Rather than stopping and deciding what would be the right thing to do, they do the wrong things faster and faster. Then they stress out over the "workload." (There is no "workload" to worry about if you are doing the right thing. There is only that thing.) And as corporate time-management specialist David Allen says of today's busy leaders: "You have more to do than you can possibly do. You just need to feel good about your choices." Multitasking is the greatest myth in modern-day business. The thinking part of the brain itself does not multitask, and so people do not really multitask. The human system is not set up that way. The brain experiences and holds only one thought at a time. Managers often think they are multitasking, but they are really just doing one thing badly and then quickly moving to another thing, doing it badly and quickly. Soon they're preoccupied with all the tasks they've touched but left incomplete. Business efficiency expert Kerry Gleeson said, "The constant, unproductive preoccupation with all the things we have to do is the single largest consumer of time and energy." Not the things we do, the things we think we still have to do. People who find the joy in leadership find ways to relax into an extremely purposeful day, goal-oriented and focused on the highest-priority activity. They relax into every given moment. Sure they get distracted, and sure, people call them and "problems" come up. But they know what to return to. Because they know their purpose. Because they chose it. That's the kind of leader that is admired and followed.

15

Look what possible

One of the best ways to motivate others is to learn from those who have motivated you. Learn from the great leaders you have had. Channel them, clone them, and incorporate them into who you are all day. Scott Richardson recalls: "The most effective, inspirational motivator that I ever had was a violin prodigy who was my violin teacher." That teacher was an associate professor of music at the University of Arizona named Rodney Mercado. I met him when I was 16 and ready to quit the violin. My mother, who desperately wanted me to be a violin player said, "Hang on, I'll find you the best teacher out there." I was skeptical. But one day, she came in and said to me, "I found him; he's the teacher of your teacher." The first time I met him, I had to audition for him. I'd never had to audition for a teacher before. Usually you'd just pay the money, and they took you. But Professor Mercado chose his students carefully, just as a great leader chooses his team. And I did the absolutely worst audition I'd ever done in my life! I thought, "Well, that sealed it. I don't have to worry about having him for my teacher." Soon after, he called me on the phone and said, "I've accepted you." And I thought, "There must be some mistake, this can't be true. I mean, my playing was so horrible, I couldn't imagine anyone accepting me based on that audition." But he had the ability to see what was possible in other people. If anyone else had heard my audition, he would have said that it was hopeless. But he heard more than the playing. He heard the possibility behind the playing. And in that, he was a profoundly great coach and leader, because one of the most vital aspects of motivating others is the ability to see what's possible instead of just seeing what's happening now. Ever since that time, I've learned not to give up on people too quickly. I've learned to look deeply and listen deeply. Soon, skills and strengths I never saw before in people would show up. I learned that people perform in response to who they think they are for us at the moment. In other words, how they think we see them is how they perform for us; therefore, if we can create a new possibility for them, and communicate that to them, their performance instantly takes off. Professor Mercado showed me another example of the power of communicating possibility when he was teaching a boy named Michael, who later became a good friend of mine. Michael was unusual. When he was in junior high, as far as I could guess, he had never ever cut his long black hair because it was longer than his sister's, which was down below her belt. And Michael always kept his hair in front of his face, so you actually couldn't see what he looked like. And he never spoke a word in public. His parents asked Professor Mercado if he would be willing to teach Michael the violin. Mercado agreed and they had lessons, but as far as any outsider could tell, it was strictly a one-way communication. Michael never responded outwardly. He never even picked up the violin! Yet Mercado continued to teach him, week after week. And then one day, when he was in 8th grade, Michael picked up the violin and started playing. And in less than a month, he was asked to solo in front of the Tucson Symphony! I could see for myself that this happened because Professor Mercado communicated to Michael (without any outward acknowledgment that communication was being received) that who Michael was (for Professor Mercado) was a virtuoso violinist. He communicated possibility. So I have always remembered from this experience that people's performance is a response to who they perceive themselves to be for us at the moment. Once we create a new possibility for those around us, and communicate to them that this new possibility is who they are for us, their performance instantly takes off. There's no better way to motivate another human being.

16

A.R.T of confrontation

One of the tricks we teach to inspire increased motivation in others is what we call "The A.R.T. of Confrontation." It shows leaders how to enjoy holding people accountable. Most managers think it's impossible to enjoy holding people accountable. They think it's the hard part of being a manager. They think it's one of the downsides—a necessary evil associated with the burden of command. Therefore you can see why they don't do a very good job of holding people accountable. Fortunately, there is an enjoyable way to do it. When you need to speak to an employee about a behavior or a performance level that is not working for you, experiment with using this A.R.T: A: First, appreciate and acknowledge the employee for who she is, what she brings to the organization, noting specific strengths and talents. Then give a very, very specific recent example of something that employee did that particularly impressed and benefited you. R: Next, restate your own commitment to that person. "I believe in you. I hired you because of what I saw in you. I see even more in you than when I hired you. I am committed to your success here. I am devoted to your career, to you being happy and fulfilled." Then, tell that employee exactly and specifically what she can count on, always, from you. List what you do, how you fight for fair pay, how you are available at all times, how you work to always get the employee the tools she needs for success, and so on. This recommitment places the conversation in the proper context. Ninety percent of managerial "reprimands" are destructive to the manager-employee relationship because they are felt to be out of context. The big picture must be established first, always. T: Last, track the agreement. You want to track the existing agreement you have with your employee (if there is one) about the matter in question. If there is no existing agreement, you should create one on the spot. Mutually authored with mutual respect. Agreements are co-creations. They are not mandates or rules. When an agreement is not being kept, both sides need to put all their cards on the table in a mutually supportive way to either rebuild the agreement or create a new agreement. People will break other people's rules. But people will keep their own agreements.

17

Feed your healthy ego

Learning to be a leader is the same process as learning to be an integrated and healthy person. —Warren Bennis

High self-esteem is our birthright. It is the core spirit inside of us. We do not need to pass a battery of humiliating tests to attain it. We need only to drop the thinking that prevents it. We need to get out of its way and let it shine, in ourselves and in others. Masterful, artful, spirited leadership has ways of bringing out the best and the highest expression of self-esteem in others. But it starts at home with me. If I'm a leader, it starts with my own self-confidence. We human beings find it easier to follow self-confident people. We are quicker to become enrolled in a project when the person enrolling us is self-confident. Most managers today don't take time to raise their own self-esteem and get centered in their personal pride of achievement. They spend too much time worrying about how they are being perceived, which results in insecurity and low self-esteem. Nathaniel Branden, in his powerful book Self-Esteem at Work (Jossey-Bass, First Edition, 1998), says it this way: A person who feels undeserving of achievement and success is unlikely to ignite high aspirations in others. Nor can leaders draw forth the best in others if their primary need, arising from their insecurities, is to prove themselves right and others wrong, in which case their relationship to others is not inspirational but adversarial. It is a fallacy to say that a great leader should be egoless. A leader needs an ego sufficiently healthy that it does not perceive itself as on trial in every encounter—is not operating out of anxiety and defensiveness—so that the leader is free to be task and results-oriented, not oriented toward self-aggrandizement or self-protection.

A healthy ego asks: What needs to be done? An insecure ego asks: How do I avoid looking bad? Build your inner strength by doing what needs to be done and then moving to the next thing that needs to be done. The less you focus on how you're coming across, the better you'll come across.

18

Hire to motivated

It sounds too simple. But the best way to have people on your team be motivated is to hire self-motivated people. But isn't that just the luck of the draw? No. There is much you can do to create this kind of team. Let's start with the hiring interview. As you conduct your hiring interview, know in advance the kinds of questions that are likely to have been anticipated by the interviewee, and therefore will only get you a role-played answer. Minimize those questions. Instead, ask questions that are original and designed to uncover the real person behind the role-player. Ask the unexpected. Keep your interviewee pleasantly off-balance. The good, motivated people will love it, and the undermotivated will become more and more uncomfortable. Know that every interviewee is attempting to role-play.They are playing the part of the person they think would get this job. We all do it in an interview. But your job is to not let it happen. One way to find the true person across from you is called layering. Layering is following up a question with an open-ended, layered addition to the question. For example: Question: Why did you leave Company X? Answer: Not enough challenges. Layered Question: Interesting, tell me more about Company X. What was it like for you there? Answer: It was pretty difficult. I wasn't comfortable. Layered Question: Why do you think it affected you that way? Answer: My manager was a micromanager. Layered Question: This is very interesting; talk more about that if you can. Basically, "layering" is a request you make that your interviewee go further and further beyond his pre-rehearsed story. You ask him to "go on," then "keep going," then "tell me more," and then "go on." Layering uncovers the real person after a while. So do questions that have not been anticipated and rehearsed for a role-play. Here's an example of a very open-ended and curious exchange: "Did you grow up here?" "No,

I grew up in Chicago." "Chicago! Did you go to high school there?" "Yes I did, Maine East High." "What was that like, going to that school?" Another example:

"How was your weekend?" "Great." "What is a typical weekend like for you?" Or another: "I see from your resume that you majored in engineering." "Yes." "If you had one thing to change about how they teach engineering, what would you change?" Or another: "If you were asked to go back to run the company you just came from, what's the first thing you would do?" Think of questions that you yourself like and are intrigued by, and keep your interviewee in uncharted waters throughout the interview. That way you get the real person to talk to you so you'll get a much better gut feeling about the person and what he or she would be like to work with. The best way to create a highly motivated team is to hire people who are already motivated people.

19

stop talking

One measure of leadership is the caliber of people who choose to follow you. —Dennis A. Peer,

Management Consultant Most job interviewers talk way too much, and they go way too soon to the question, "Well, is there anything you would like to know about us?"

Learn to stop doing that. That's your ego being expressed, not a good interview technique. People who have not done their homework and who are not masterful interviewers will always end up interviewing themselves and talking about their company. Totally unproductive. They get uncomfortable asking lots of questions so they quickly start talking about the history of the company, their own history there, and many personal convictions and opinions. In this, they are wasting their time. In five months, they will be wringing their hands and tearing their hair out because somehow they let a problem employee and chronic complainer fly in under the radar. And it will keep happening until you learn to interview. Remember: no talking. Your job is to intuit the motivational level of the person across from you. You can only do that by letting her answer question after question. It takes more courage, imagination, and preparation to ask a relentless number of questions than it does to chat. Great leaders are great recruiters. In sports and in life. As a leader, you're only as good as your people. Hire the best. Dale Dauten, often called the Obi-Wan Kenobi of business consultants, said, "When I did the research that led to my book The Gifted Boss (William Morrow, First Edition, 1999), I found that great bosses spend little time trying to mold employees into greatness, but instead devote extraordinary efforts to spotting and courting exceptionally capable employees. Turns out that the best management is finding employees that don't need managing."

20

Be limitless ,refuse Limitation

Leaders don't create followers, they create more leaders. —Tom Peters, Author/Business Consultant Your people limit themselves all the time. They put up false barriers and struggle with imaginary problems. One of your skills as a leader will be to show your people that they can accomplish more than they think they can. In fact, they may someday be a leader like you are. One of the reasons your people will wind up admiring you is that you always see their potential. You always see the best side of them, and you tell them about it. It could be that you are the first person in that employee's life to ever believe in him. And because of you, he becomes more capable than he thought he was, and he loves you for that, even though your belief in him sometimes makes him uncomfortable. That discomfort may return every time you ask him to stretch. But you don't care. You press on with your belief in him, stretching him, growing him. One of the greatest leadership gurus of American business was Robert Greenleaf. He developed the concept of "servant leadership." A leader is one who serves those following, serving them every step of the way, especially by bringing out the best in them, and refusing to buy their limitations as achievers. Your people may be flawed as people, but as achievers, they are certainly not.Greenleaf said, "Anybody could lead perfect people— if there were any. But there aren't any perfect people. And parents who try to raise perfect children are certain to raise neurotics. "It is part of the enigma of human nature that the 'typical' person—immature, stumbling, inept, lazy—is capable of great dedication and heroism if wisely led. The secret of team-building is to be able to weld a team of such people by lifting them up to grow taller than they would otherwise be."

21

play both good and bad cop

If you are an effective motivator of others, then you know how to play "good cop, bad cop." And you know that you don't need two people to play it. A true motivator plays both roles. Good Cop: Nurturing, mentoring, coaching, serving, and supporting your people all the way. Keeping your word every time. Removing obstacles to success. Praising and acknowledging all the way. Leading through positive reinforcement of desired behavior, because you're a true leader who knows that you get what you reward. Bad Cop: Bad to the bone. No compromise about people keeping their promises to you, even promises about performance. No room for complaints and excuses as substitutions for conversations about promises not being kept. No respect for whiners and people who do not make their numbers. No "wiggle room" for the lazy. Clarity, conviction, determination. All cards on the table. No covert messages. In your face: "I believe in you. I know what you can do. When you don't do it, you let yourself and the team down. I won't allow that. Time to wake up." Obviously you don't call on Bad Cop every day. Only after every Good Cop approach is exhausted. But Bad Cop can be a great wake-up call to someone who has never been challenged in life to be the best she can be. And once the Bad Cop session is over, and the person is back in the game, giving it a good effort, bring Good Cop back right away to complete the process.

22

Don't Go Crazy

The older I get the more wisdom I find in the ancient rule of taking first things first. A process which often reduces the most complex human problem to a manageable proportion. —Dwight D. Eisenhower

When I'm thinking about seven things rather than one, I'm trying to keep them in my head while I'm trying to listen to you, but I really can't because I just thought of three more things that I need to attend to when you leave, which I hope will be soon. So I look at my watch a couple of times while you're talking to me, because mentally I'm on the run, and I'm a type-A go-go-guy, doing a million things! But what I'm not seeing is that my very fragile relationship with you is being destroyed by this approach. It's being destroyed a little bit at a time, because the main message I'm sending to you and everyone else on my team is that I'm really stressed, and it's crazy here inside my head. I even tell my family, "It's crazy at work. I want to spend more time with you, but it's crazy right now. Just crazy at the office." Well, it's not crazy. You're crazy. You need to be honest about it. It's not crazy; it's just work. It's just a business. "It's-crazy-around-here" managers keep throwing up their hands, saying, "What? She's leaving us? Why? She's quitting? Oh no, you can't trust anybody these days. Get her in here, we need to save this. Cancel my meetings, cancel my calls, I want to find out why she's leaving." Well, she's leaving for this reason: You only spoke to her for a maximum of three minutes in any single conversation over the past year. You may have spoken to her 365 times, but it was only for three minutes. This is not a professional relationship. It's drive-by management. And whether the go-go manager likes it or not, creating great relationships is how careers are built, how businesses are built, and how great teams are built. Usually, people who think they admire or in a certain, frightened, way "respect" their multitasking managers, admit that they feel less secure because of all that is "crazy." When they meet with that manager, the manager says to them, "Okay, come on in, I know you need to see me. Get in here, I have to take this call. It's crazy. I've got to be in a meeting in two minutes, and there's an e-mail I'm waiting for, so you'll forgive me if I jump on that when it comes in, but just step in here for a second. I know you had something on your mind. So please, ah, talk to me...oh, excuse me." When we can get a manager to experiment with slowing down and becoming focused on each conversation as a way to approach his or her day, they're really amazed. If they do it for a week, they call back and say, "Unbelievably, I got more understanding of my people this week than in all my previous weeks on this job." Yet it could be different. Life could slow down and become excellent. Because often, when they do slow down and look at the next urgent task in front of them, it occurs to them that someone else would love to do this task. Not only that, but someone else would be flattered to do this. "They would enjoy hearing of the trust I have in them by asking them to take this over and get it done, and done well, because I like the way they do things." There are so many things that can be delegated and passed on to others, but only if you regain your sanity and slow down. One of the best ways to motivate others is to give them more interesting things to do. Especially things that free up your own time. That's time you can use to build a motivated team. It doesn't have to be crazy around here. You can put an end to that.

Unconsciously, managers without leadership habits will often seek, above all else, to be liked. Rather than holding people accountable, they let them off the hook. They give non-performers the uneasy feeling that everything's fine. They are managers who seek approval rather than success. But this habit has a severe consequence. It leads to a lack of trust in the workplace. Lack of trust: the most common problem "issue" on employee surveys. A true leader does not focus on trying to be liked. A true leader focuses on the practices and communications that lead to being respected. It's a completely different goal that leads to completely different results. (I am not motivated by you because I like you; I am motivated by you because I respect you.) The core internal question that the leader returns to is, "If I were being managed by me, what would I most need from my leader right now?" The answer to that question varies, but most often is: 1. The truth, as soon as you know the truth. 2. Full and complete communication about what's going on with me and with us. 3. Keeping all promises, especially the small ones ("I'll get back to you by tomorrow with that") consistently, even fanatically. Not some promises, not a high percentage of promises, not a good college try, but all promises. When a promise cannot be kept (especially a small one), an immediate apology, update, and a new and better promise is issued.

A true leader does not try to become everybody's big buddy, although he or she values being upbeat and cheerful in communication. A true leader is not overly concerned with always being liked, and is even willing to engage in very uncomfortable conversations in the name of being straight and thorough. A true leader sees this aspect of leadership in very serious, adult terms, and does not try to downplay responsibility for leadership. True leaders do not try to form inappropriate private friendships with members of the team they are paid to lead. A true leader enjoys all the elements of accountability and responsibility and transforms performance measurement and management into an above-board business adventure.

23

Do the worst first

The best way out is always through. —Robert Frost

The number-one topic that leaders ask us to speak about these days is: How do you motivate others when you have poor time-management? This was true of Carlos, who headed up a team of brokers. "With everything that's flying at me, everything that's coming in, all the calls that I get, all the obligations that I have, I could really use another 10 hours in my day," Carlos said. We laughed: "This is true of everyone, Carlos. Stop thinking you are unique. Re-program and bring yourself into focus. Reboot your mind. Start over."All talented people in this global market have more to do than they have time to do. That's not really a problem. It's an exciting fact of life. "But it's very, very tempting to cave in to a sense of being overwhelmed," Carlos said. "It's tempting to get into that victim mindset of being 'swamped.'" "True enough. So regroup and get the view from 30,000 feet. Rise up. Lift yourself up!" "But the truth is, I am swamped," Carlos almost yelled out. "There's nothing I can do. I'm overwhelmed. How can anyone manage this team when you've got all this stuff going on? And right when you think you're getting ahead of it, you get a call, you get an e-mail, you get another request, there's another program that has to be implemented, there's another form that has to be filled out, and I'm about to throw up my hands and say, 'How do I do this?'" "Carlos, listen. Get a grip for now. The simplest system that you can come up with for time management will serve you as a leader. Keep it simple." "Why does it have to be simple?" Carlos asked. "It seems like I need a more complex solution to a complex set of challenges." "Because no matter what you do, you can't stop this one truth about leadership: You are going to be hounded, you're going to be barraged, and you're going to be interrupted. And there are two reactions you can choose between to address this leadership fact of life." Carlos said nothing. "You could just become a victim and say, 'I can't handle it, there's just too much to do.' That takes no imagination, it takes no courage, and it's simply the easiest way to go— to complain about your situation. Maybe even complain to other people, other leaders, other managers, other family members; they will all sympathize with you and might even say, 'You've got to get out of that business.'" Carlos started nodding in agreement. "That happens," Carlos said. "But that doesn't help me enjoy my job: to have friends and family feeding back to me that I ought to get out of the business. That makes it twice as hard." "Right! So there's another way to go, and this is by keeping the simplest time-management system possible in your life. This is the one that we recommend, and it's the one that most leaders have had the most luck with. It's so simple, you can boil it down to two words, if you have to. The words are these: worst first!" "Worst first?" "Exactly. Write it down!" We worked with Carlos for a long time to get him to see that the best way to manage his time was not to think of it as managing time, but to think of it as managing priorities. Because he can't really "manage time." He can't add any more time to his day. But he can manage the priorities and the things that he chooses to do. "Worst first," Carlos said. "Explain it again. What does it mean?" "Write down on a piece of paper all the things you'd like to do in the upcoming day, Carlos. Maybe you were jotting them down last night, but these are all things that you know that you would like to do. The list doesn't have to be perfect. It can be all kinds of shorthand, and little pictures and drawings, all over a scratched-up piece of paper. Then you choose, among all these things, the one thing that's the most challenging and important. The one thing you wish you didn't have to do." "How do I know for sure what that is? And how will this, in the long run, improve the motivation of my people? Isn't that your area of specialty?" "Yes it is, but until you get this down, you won't motivate anyone. You have to have a secure place to come from. An organized place inside yourself." "Okay, okay, I know that, but how do I choose the one thing to focus on?" "What is that one thing that you're most likely to put off? What's your most important thing to do, the thing that really needs to be done; not necessarily the most urgent thing, but the most important?" "Oh," said Carlos, "I think I'm seeing this. That thing that pains me most to think of. That's what I select to do first." "That's it." Most managers are like Carlos. They don't have a simple system. They just respond to whatever's most urgent. All day they wonder, "What has to be addressed right now?" And a lot of time, the urgent little things that come up as an answer to that question are really small. They're nitpicky things, just hassles. "But don't the little things have to be done?" Carlos asked. "Yeah, they have to be done, but in the meantime you're leaving important things behind. Many times, it is even more effective to turn off your phones, get away from your e-mail, select something that's important, and do that until it's complete, and let the urgent go hang." "I do know that there's always something that eats at the back of my mind," Carlos said. "It keeps coming up, I keep thinking about it. It gets in the way of the things I'm doing." "Now you're on the right track, Carlos! You can't focus in a relaxed and cheerful way on the things you are doing because in the back of your mind, this important thing is there. When you go home at night, the thing that makes you the most weary, the most under-the-weather, and most gives you the sense of not having had a good day, is that one thing you didn't do, but wish you had." "Right. Boy do I know." "So this is what you want to get into the category of Worst First: You want to pick that one thing that's hardest to do, that you would love to have finished and behind you. You want to make it number one. First priority. Nothing gets done until that gets done." Weeks went by, and Carlos struggled with the system, but finally warmed up to it after a lot of practice. After Carlos had finally made the "worst first" system into a habit, he felt a freedom he never felt before. People around him were inspired by how liberated he was becoming every day from having done the hardest thing first. Carlos would handle his biggest thing as his first thing, and then live like the rest of the day was a piece of cake. His energy soared. Soon he was teaching others the same system. He called a few months later to give an update on his newly centered life in leadership. "I am really freed up by this," Carlos said. "If someone says to me, 'Will you sit down and talk to me about this issue?' and I have done my worst thing already, I can say 'Sure, how much time do you need? Let's talk.'"

24

Try to Experiment

Don't be too timid and squeamish about your actions. All life is an experiment. The more experiments you make, the better. —Ralph Waldo Emerson One of the most common complaints of today's executives is this: The people that they supervise hate to make changes though they are constantly being required to in this highly competitive business environment. The executives then tear out their hair trying to get the needed changes accomplished. The way we respond is that it may feel difficult to encourage people to change. But try this possibility: People may not like to change, but they do love to experiment! As business consultant and journalist Dale Dauten has observed, "Experimentation never fails. When you try something and it turns out to be a lousy idea, you never really go back to where you started. You learned something. If nothing else, it makes you appreciate what you were doing before. So I think it's true that experiments never fail." So in the businesses that we coach, there are never any changes. However, our clients' businesses are constantly experimenting to find what works better for the employees, the business, and the customer. The executives simply tell their teams, "This is an experiment to see if it works better for you and our customers. If it does, great, we are going to continue doing it. If it doesn't, then we will modify it or get rid of it." And as long as you monitor it and get feedback, you'll find that the old-fashioned resistance to change melts away because your employees really do enjoy a good experiment.

25

communicate consciously

Drowning in data, yet starved of information. —Ruth Stanat, Global Business Consultant

We live in the information age. Your people use their minds creatively and productively throughout the day. They aren't just digging tunnels; they all communicate for a living. Now, more than ever before, communication is their lifeblood. It is the lifeblood of every organization. Yet many organizations leave most of their communication to chance, to "common sense," or to old traditions that no longer function to keep everyone informed and included. Communication is the source of trust and respect within each organization, so let's put all our cards on the table as often as possible. When we increase our awareness of communication, communication is enhanced. When we take full responsibility for how we communicate, the organization is enhanced. Leadership authority Warren Bennis says, "Good leaders make their people see they are at the very heart of things, not at the periphery. Everyone feels that he or she makes a difference to the success of the organization. When that happens people feel centered and that gives their work meaning."

26
Score your performance

Performance is your reality. Forget everything else. —Harold Geneen, CEO, ITT Can you imagine playing a game in which you don't know how it's scored? Or competing in front of judges when you don't know their criteria? And the judges are not going to tell you for a long time how you did? That would be an athlete's nightmare. We sat in a meeting run by Megan who was having a hard time motivating her team to hit the company's expected goals. "Exactly how are we doing right now?" her team member Clarence asked Megan from the end of the round table around which we were all sitting for the team meeting. "Oh, I don't know, Clarence," said Megan. "I haven't looked at the printout yet. I have a sense that we are doing pretty well this month, but I haven't gotten to the numbers yet." You could see the look on Clarence's face. It was a cross between disappointment and pain. Later, we met with Megan alone and explained to her why she needed to change her approach immediately if she had any hope of motivating Clarence and his teammates. She had to know the score. "I just don't enjoy numbers," Megan said. "I never have. I'm not a numbers kind of person." "Whether you enjoy numbers or not, if you're in a leadership position, it is imperative to be the numbers person for your team. There's no way you're going to have amotivated team here, Megan, until you do your homework, put the numbers in front of you, and talk about those numbers when you talk to your people. If you're their coach, and you are, then you talk about the game and the score." "Well, I played a little basketball in high school," Megan said. "Maybe I can relate it to that." "Imagine your basketball coach during a game. Your team comes to the sideline, it's late in the game, and your coach says, 'Now I haven't looked at the scoreboard for a while, so I don't know how many points we're down, or are we up? Anyway, here are some plays that I think we ought to run after the time-out.'" Megan smiled and said, "That would be a coach that I wouldn't have any confidence in whatsoever!" "Why not, Megan?" Megan said nothing. "Aren't you that coach, Megan?" Megan said, "I think I see what you mean. My best coaches were people who rewarded numbers and got excited." "Right! Great leaders are the same. They are leaders who call team members and say, 'Hey, I just got your numbers for last week. Wow, that's better than you've done all year!' These are the leaders people love to follow, because they always know whether they are winning or losing. They always know the score." We reminded Megan that earlier in her team meeting she had said to her group, "Well, you guys are really trying hard and I know you are making the effort. I drove by last night and I saw your lights on late, so I really admire what you guys are doing. You're really giving it the old college try." We told her that she might be on the wrong course with that approach. "What was wrong with saying that?" Megan asked. "It's wrong because respect for achievement is replaced by respect for 'trying.' Megan, listen, we have a phrase in our society's language that sums it up. When someone is willfully obtuse and ineffective, we say that person doesn't 'know the score.' Why? Because 'knowing the score' is the first step in all achievement." What we wanted Megan to see was that this mistake of hers was immediately correctable. It was only the mistake of not looking over some numbers before sending an e-mail or making a call. But that one little mistake will give her team the impression that they're here for reasons other than winning and achieving precise goals. The coach has to be the one to explain to the team with tremendous precision exactly what the score is, exactly how much time is left, and exactly how the strategy is based on those numbers. When you have a numbers-based team, you know when you are winning, you know when you've had a good day, you know when you're having a good run, and you know when you are not. That creates a wonderful sense that there is no hidden agenda from this leader. So look for ways, as you communicate with your people, to improve and increase the way they are measured and, especially, to increase the consciousness of that measurement. But it has to come from you. You can't wait around for the company policy to shift. That's what most people do. They wait for their own management to come up with some kind of new system, new scorebooks, new posters, something like that. But don't do that. Don't wait. Have it come from you. It has to be your personal innovation to find more ways to keep score. That way, people will link it to you and know how much it means to you. Is there anything that you want improved? Find ways to track it, to keep score. The love of games that is in every human being is something that you can tap into. The more you measure things, the more motivated your people are to win those games.

27

Manage the Fundamental

Show me a man who cannot bother to do little things and I'll show you a man who cannot be trusted to do big things. —Lawrence D. Bell, Founder, Bell Aircraft The Rodney Mercado motivational methods are not only the most effective methods for teaching music, but for anything else. Professor Mercado was a genius in 10 different fields, including mathematics, economics, sociology, anthropology, and music history. Scott recalls: Once, I was surprised to be getting an economics lesson inside my music lesson. Mercado turned to me and said, "Well, Scott, you know, math is very, very simple. It's all based on addition. But most people lose sight of that. So if you learn how to do one plus one equals two, everything in math flows from that. Everything." He was always focusing on fundamentals. Like the time he came to assist our chamber group in preparing to perform a piece. Under his guidance, we spent the entire hour working on the first two measures of this piece. We kept going over and over them, and each time he would ask us to explore a new possibility. "How would you like to create more sound here?" he would ask. And then he would give us ideas on how we could possibly do that. And by the end of the hour, all we had done was work on two measures of a piece that probably had 80 measures of music. Then, at the very end, he said, "Okay, now let's play the whole thing." The entire performance and our entire group were transformed. We played the whole thing beautifully! That showed me the power of fundamentals. Don't gloss over them. Slow your people down and do things step by step, getting the basics right, getting the fundamentals in place. We were coaching a client recently in his companywide managers' meeting, and two people didn't show up on time for the meeting. The CEO wanted to rush through the meeting and "talk to the people who didn't show up" later. But we slowed him down and had the whole group focus, slowly and fundamentally, on how to handle this tardiness and absenteeism and lack of commitment from these two managers. In the process, we had a number of breakthrough moments for other managers on the nature of commitment, and a newer, more creative policy emerged.

28

Motivate with doing

People can be divided into two classes: those who go ahead and do something, and those people who sit still and inquire, why wasn't it done the other way? —Oliver Wendell Holmes Most managers don't do things according to priority— they do things according to feelings. That's how their day is run. (This, by the way, is exactly how infants live. They live from feeling to feeling. Do they feel like crying? Do they feel like laughing? Do they feel like drooling? That's an infant's life.) Professional managers fall into two categories: doers and feelers. Doers do what needs to be done to reach a goal that they themselves have set. They come to work having already planned out what needs to be done. Feelers, on the other hand, do what they feel like doing. Feelers take their emotional temperature throughout the day, checking in on themselves, figuring out what they feel like doing right now. Their lives, their outcomes, their financial security are all dictated by the fluctuation of their feelings. Their feelings will change constantly, of course, so it's hard for a feeler to follow anything through to a successful conclusion. Their feelings are changed by many things: biorhythms, gastric upset, a strong cup of coffee, an annoying call from home, a rude waitress at lunch, a cold, a bit of a headache, a thought. Those are the dictating forces, the commanders, of a feeler's life. A doer already knows in advance how much time will be spent on the phone, how much in the field, what employees will be cultivated that day, what relationships will be strengthened, what communications need to be made. Doers use a three-step system to guarantee success: 1. They figure out what they want to achieve. 2. They figure out what needs to be done to achieve it. 3. They do it. This is not a theory, this is the actual observed system used by all super achievers without fail. A feeler is adrift in a mysterious life of unexpected consequences and depressing problems. A feeler asks, “Do I feel like making my phone calls now?” “Do I feel like writing that thank you note?” “Do I feel like dropping in on that person right now?” If the answer is no, then the feeler keeps going down the list, asking, “Do I feel like doing something else?” A feeler lives inside that line of inquiry all day long. By contrast, a doer has high self-esteem. A doer enjoys many satisfactions throughout the day, even though some of them were preceded by discomfort. A feeler is almost always trying to be comfortable, but never really satisfied. A doer knows the true, deep joy that only life’s super achievers know. A feeler believes that joy is for children, and that life for an adult is an ongoing hassle. A doer experiences more and more power every year of life. A feeler feels less and less powerful as the years go on. Your ability to motivate others increases exponentially as your reputation as a doer increases. You also get more and more clarity about who the doers and feelers are on your own team. Then, as you model and reward the doing, you also begin to inspire the feelers on your team to become doers.

29

Know your people strength

Know your people's strengths. It's the fundamental business insight that inspired the book Good to Great by Jim Collins (HarperBusiness, 2001). And this idea of going from good to great also applies to the people you motivate. It's far more effective to build on their strengths than to worry too much about their weaknesses. The first step is to really know their strengths so you can help them to express them even more. Most managers spend way too much time, especially in the world of sales, trying to fix what's wrong. Your people may identify negative things and say, "Oh, I'm not good at this. I need to change that. And I'm not very good on the phone. I need to fix that...." But listen to their voice tones when they say these things! They'll always sound depressed and world-weary. Here's the simple formula (and once we recognize this formula, we can do some wonderful things): If people focus on what's wrong with them, just focusing on that puts them in a bad mood. People grimly, glumly, confront with a kind of morbid honesty, what's wrong. And the voice tones go down, because the enthusiasm goes down, and the dreariness sets in. And pretty soon, they're putting off activities. They're procrastinating. They're saying, "This makes me uncomfortable. I don't even like thinking about this right now. For some reason (I don't know why, I was in a good mood before I started...), I'm not in the mood to work on this. I can tell that I can't work on this problem until I feel a little more energy. I mean, you can't work on something when there's no energy to work." We went into a computer company and listened as the manager, Matt, talked about his team. "I wish my salespeople would do more research before their sales calls," Matt said. And then when we sat down with one of Matt's salespeople, Byron, he said, "Yeah, that's something I'm not very good at." "Okay, you're not very good at that. So let's move on." "No, no, I need to fix that," said Byron. "That's something that needs to be fixed. I need to get better. Why don't you coach me? How do I get better at that?" And we could hear his low voice tone. We knew Byron would never get better at that because of the negative mindset the very subject put him in. To really take something on and to grow and strengthen it, people need to be in an upbeat, positive mood. People need to have energy. That's when they're at their best.

"So, when will my people have energy?" manager Matt asked us after we explained the concept of moods to him. "They get energy when they think about the things they're really good at in sales. Have them ask themselves, 'What am I really good at? What are my strengths?' The minute they start focusing on those things, their energy will pick up. Their self-esteem will pick up. Their enthusiasm will pick up." That's where the fastest infusion of productivity always comes from. First, you find what this person is good at, and then you move good to great. When we worked with Matt's salesperson Byron, we said, "Okay, Byron, forget about your weaknesses, forget about what you're not good at. That's probably all you've been thinking about for a few months, right?" "Right," said Byron. "You know, my manager counsels me on it. I've had things written up about it. I've been given activities to do to correct it. But the problem is, I just go deeper, and I don't produce." "Listen, Byron, set those activities aside. Forget about all the problems that need to be fixed. We're not going to fix anything for now. We want an infusion, we want a stimulus. We want a burst of sales to take you out of the cellar and put you up there where you belong in the upper rankings of the salespeople. Later, when we have the luxury, and we're bored, and we can't figure out what to do in coaching sessions, we may take a weakness and play around with it, for the pure fun of it. But for now, we're not going to do it. Here's what we're going to do. We're going to acknowledge one thing: You're not going to be great at anything until you enjoy it. We want to find out what you're already good at, and we want to build on that."

"Well, one of my strengths is in-person," said Byron. "I love to be in-person. I'm bad on the phone, I'm bad with faxes, I'm bad with e-mail. But in-person, I can just close deals, I can talk, I can expand, I can upsell, I can cross-sell...." "Okay, great. So rather than fix the phone thing and fix the e-mail thing, let's leave those aside for the moment. Only use them if you must to get an appointment. Don't use them to sell anything. We want to increase what you're good at. Get out there, sit with people. Keep increasing that and get even better at it. Don't say 'I'm already good at it, and that's that.' Of course you're good at it. But the way you're going to be really tremendous in this field is to turn good into great, to get great at that thing, because you're more than two-thirds of the way there. Because you're already good at it." What we wanted to steer Byron away from is this thought: "Well, I'm already good at it, that's sort of natural, that comes easy to me. That's sort of cheating when I do a lot of that. What I really need to do is work at what I'm bad at." To be great motivators, we need to look at human behavior differently. We've been taught the wrong way since we were young! If we got an A in science, but we flunked English, our parents said, "Hey, I don't care about your other grades, what you really need to do is work hard on your English, because you flunked it. So you're going to focus your life on English for a while." All of our lives, we've been taught that the way to succeed is to take something that you're not good at and change it. Take your weaknesses and spend time with them so that you can bring your weaknesses up to "normal."

Do you know how little an effect it has on someone's productivity if they take their weaknesses and work hard and finally bring them from "subnormal" to "normal"? All throughout life we've been taught that when we're good at something, it just means it's innate. Our parents say, "Oh, he's really good at the piano. He must have gotten that from his grandfather, he must have inherited that, he's got a natural talent at that." So we're taught not to focus on it. We're taught that that will be okay by itself. People tell us, "You really need to put your attention on all the things you're bad at!" Jennifer was on a sales staff we were coaching, and she was kind of intimidated because the sales staff had a lot of flashy, good-looking, well-dressed fraternity-type guys and sorority-type girls on it. Jennifer was more of a shy person. She was very bright and very compassionate, but she just couldn't make herself do things the way the other salespeople did. And so she was frustrated, and all she tried to do was work on her weaknesses, and whenever we met her, she would bring in this long list of things she wasn't any good at. "These are the things I want to talk about," Jennifer said. "These are the top seven things I'm terrible at." "Throw that list out." "What?" "We don't care about that list. We really don't. You wouldn't be here if you didn't have the basic skills to be here. So stop it. Here's what we'd like you to do. Think back for a little while. Think about your life. When were you really happy? If you can look back and get in touch with moments in your life when you were really happy, it's going to give us some clues about where to go from here."

"Well, I was a waitress not too long ago, before I came here," Jennifer said. "There was a restaurant that I worked in that, originally, I didn't like, but finally just loved. I really enjoyed it. It was like I was in heaven, I just got so good at it. I was serving customers and I was taking their orders and I got the biggest tips of anybody there. It was just wonderful. It felt like a dance, it felt like a musical. And also, the money coming in to me was greater than anyone else there." "We've hit on something here!" "Well, I can't do that," Jennifer said. "I've got bills to pay, I've got kids. I can't go back to that. There's not enough money there, no matter how good you are. I've got to do this. I've got to get the big accounts. I've got to get the big commissions I know I can make." "So we're going to do that. But we're not going to do it from being a back-slapping, flashy salesperson. We're going to go with your strength." "Well, my strength is waiting on tables and serving people." "Yes! So that's what you're going to do. That's who you're going to be. You're going to serve. You're going to take orders. You're going to present menus. You're going to explain what the dishes are like. You're going to ask clients what they like. You're going to give them options, and that same person you were in the restaurant, you're going to be in this selling situation. You're going to tap into that same love of serving and presenting options, and fulfilling orders. That's going to be who you are, but you're going to do it in this context, selling this product. And when you get on the phone, you're going to be that way, you're going to be the person who wants to know how you can help. Not a salesperson. Not a salesperson at all. You will use all the words you used when you were a happy waitress. 'You're not quite ready? I'd be glad to come back. Take your time. I want you to know what's here. I want you to know what the specials are, so you can make your decision.' And come from that point of view. That's who you are. That's a way of being that you loved being. And you can be that here. You can serve rather than sell, and it will work for you." Two or three months later, Jennifer was doing extremely well. She had made a remarkable breakthrough. She came at the whole job from a completely different place. She took what she loved to do the most, and she did that all day. She took what she already knew she was good at, she took a strength, and she moved it from good to great.

30

Debate Yourself

All it might take is half a day to catch everything up, sort everything out, clean everything away, and be ready to begin next week with a whole new lease on life, staying organized as you go. But still you resist.You know you will never "find time" to do that half a day of reorganization. Therefore, you must make time. Winners make time to do what's really beneficial and important to them. Losers keep trying to "find time." When you hear a pessimistic manager say, "I'm sorry I didn't get back to you, Dave. I was swamped yesterday," that swamped feeling has become reality. But being "swamped" is just an interpretation. If that manager was locked in solitary confinement for five years, and somebody offered him this job where they had a lot of phone calls and things to do, would they call it "being swamped"? They would call it being wonderfully busy. They would call it absolute heaven. So which is it? Swamped or busy? A woman in one of our workshops a year ago said, "My job is a total nightmare. It is hell on earth. The fact that I even show up for it is surprising to me—it is an absolute nightmare." "What is the nightmare?" "Well, I've got people calling in, I've got two different bosses telling me what to do. I've got an in-box stacked like this high, and I go home from work stressed out." "Okay, what if we were to introduce you to a woman from Rwanda whose husband has been dead for two years and who has had to eat out of garbage cans to live, do you think you could persuade her that your job is a nightmare? Would she like trading lives with you? Would your job be a nightmare to that woman?" "Oh, no, not to her it wouldn't be a nightmare. It would be the greatest blessing." "So, is your job a nightmare? A nightmare is only a nightmare in your own thinking. It's a perception. You can choose another if you want. You can choose another job, or you can choose another perception. You are free." Be willing to teach your people how to debate themselves. Forget that it's supposed to be a sign of insanity to be talking to yourself. Because the truth is that when we question our own thinking, we start to elevate to new levels of thinking. We start to really accomplish things if we have enough courage to question our own thinking. Here are some questions we might want to ask ourselves, for beginners: "Is that really true? Is my manager really out to get me? Is this really happening? Is this really a bad opportunity? It might be, but is it really? What else could I say about it? What would be a more useful way to interpret it?" We can teach people to question everything they have labeled as negative. Be ruthless with yourself, too, as you debate the chaos that builds up in your life. Simplify your life to feel your full power. When Vince Lombardi was asked why his world-champion football team had the simplest offensive system in all of football, his response was, "It's hard to be aggressive when you're confused."

31

Lead with language

We once worked with a group of managers who managed various teams in a company plagued with low morale. The teams were grumbling, and exulting in victim language. But once we suggested different words and language for the managers to use in team meetings, everything began to change. Their people became more self-motivated. As the psychological turnaround advanced, the managers began to open their meetings by asking who had an acknowledgment—"Who would like to acknowledge someone else right now?"—and the talk began to swing to appreciation, instead of to complaint and criticism. And all of a sudden, the mood of the meetings changed. Instead of focusing on problems, and getting stuck there, the leaders would learn to say, "What opportunities do you see?" And just by saying that enough times, a different kind of energy would emerge. Different than the low-morale days when the leaders used to say, "What are the problems? What do we have to get through? Who's to blame?" When managers asked, "What can we get from this?" results changed faster. "We had a tough week last week. Let's go around the table. What can we learn from that? What are some new systems we might put in? If that comes up again, what would be a great way of dealing with it? How can we have fun with this in the future?" The managers got the victim language out of their systems. They got stronger by using, "What do we want? What's our intention? What's our goal? What outcome would we love to see?" Every time victim language was replaced by the language of intention, different results occurred. Some of the most dramatic results: 1. Turnover decreased. 2. Absenteeism decreased. 3. Spirit and morale improved. 4. Productivity increased. And all that happened with language. Words mean things. Words that form thoughts create things. Ancient scriptures say, "In the beginning, there was the word."

And there's a lot of modern-day truth to that. Words start things going. Change a single word in what you say, and you can scare a child. One scary word can make a child shake and cry. Change that word back, and the child is fine. Words communicate pictures, energy, emotions, possibilities, and fears. Words can scare an employee, too. Sometimes victims try to be leaders, but can't. That's because they think they ought to do it. But the leadership spirit is not accessed that way. It's a graceful spirit, not a heavy burden. This type of language won't get you there: "I should be more of a leader." Any time a victim finds out about leadership language, and then says, "You know, I really should be more of a leader," that's simply more victim language! That drives the person deeper down into victim feelings. Why should you be more of a leader? "Well, I guess people would like me more. They would approve of me more." Who cares what other people think? What do you want? Leadership is based on personal, internal intention. It's living a life that has clarity of purpose at the center of it. Victimization is not based on intention. Victimization is based on being a victim of circumstance and other people's opinion. The victim is constantly obsessed with what other people think.

"Well, what would my wife think if I did that? What would my kids think? What would my boss think? What would the people think if they saw me singing in my car? If a person pulls up next to me, what's he gonna think?" Obsessing about what other people think throughout the day is the fastest way to lose your enthusiasm for life. It's the fastest way to lose that basic energy that gets everything done that you've ever been proud of. You notice that children don't seem to have that worry. Most children, when they're in the middle of something they really love, seem to forget that anybody is watching them, and even forget that there's a world out there. They just get swept away. Good leaders do the same thing.

32

Use Positive Reinforcement

The first duty of a leader is optimism. How does your subordinate feel after meeting with you? Does he feel uplifted? If not, you are not a leader. —Field Marshall Montgomery Nobody remembers it. Everybody seems to forget it. But positive reinforcement trumps negative criticism every time. It doesn't matter if you are training dolphins or motivating your team members, positive reinforcement is the way to go. You don't see trainers at Sea World beating the dolphins with baseball bats when they don't jump through the right hoops. You see them, instead, giving them little fish when they do jump through. Why can't we remember that? We're too busy chasing down problems and then criticizing the problematic people who created the problems. That's how most managers "lead." But that's a habit trap. And like any other habit trap, there are certain small behaviors that will remove you from that trap. For example, you will want to pause a moment before e-mailing or calling any one of your team players. You will want to take a moment. You want to decide what small appreciation you can communicate to them. You will want to always realize that positive reinforcement is powerful when it comes to guiding and shaping human performance. This revelation continues to surprise us, because we have been trained by our society to identify what's wrong and fix it. There's a better way: Find out what's right and reward it. A very surprised Napoleon once said, "The most amazing thing I have learned about war is that men will die for ribbons."

33

Teach your people no power

The tragedy of a disempowered, weak-willed life extends to all aspects of work.

Unless you change it. Tina reports to you. And one of the things she reports to you is that she is stressed out and incapable of doing all of her work. After a long talk about her life on the job, it becomes clear that Tina has no goals, plans, or commitments. It is no wonder, therefore, that Tina allows people to waste her time. People that Tina doesn't even care about keep taking up her time. She can't say no to them only because she hasn't said yes to anything else. You talk to her. "The greatest value of planning and goal-setting is that it gives you your own life to live. It puts you back in charge. It allows you to focus on what's most important to you. So you won't walk around all week singing the Broadway song, 'I'm Just A Girl Who Can't Say No.'" You begin to sing that song to her. She begs you to stop. "Okay, how do I turn it around?" Tina asks you. "How do I learn to say no?" "Ask yourself these questions: 'What goals are most important to me? And how much time do I give them? What people are most important to me? And how much time do I give them?'" We hear many complaints from people in business who are going through the same kind of scattered lives. It's as if they're dying from a thousand tiny distractions. They report a life of being constantly drained by other people's requests. People poking their heads in all day saying, "Gotta minute? Gotta minute?"

Slam the door on those poking heads. Those incessant talking heads give you a life in which you have not learned to say no. Once you learn it, teach it to your people, too. Make it an honorable thing. Your people's access to focused work will depend on their willingness to develop a little-used muscle that we call the No Muscle. If they never use this muscle, it won't perform for them when the chips are down. It will be too weak to work. Any request by any coworker or relative will pull them from the mission. The key to teaching your people to develop the No Muscle is to first develop their Yes Muscle. If they will say yes to the things that are important to them, then saying no to what's not important will get easier and easier. Help them verbalize what they want. Make them say it out loud. "Tina, you need to know what you want, know it in advance, and chances are you'll get it. It's easy to say no to something if you've already said yes to something better."

34

Keep your people thinking friendly

Our customers are the origin, the originating source, of all the money we have and all the things we own. It's not the company that pays us, it's the customer. The company just passes the customer's money along to us. When we take a vacation, it's important to realize that the customer has paid for it. When we send a child to college, it's with our customer's money! Sam Walton built his Wal-Mart empire knowing that there was always only one boss: the customer. He believes that the customer has the power to fire everyone in the company simply by spending his money somewhere else. Why not begin motivating our people accordingly? Why not show our people the joy of treating that customer relationship as a real and genuine friendship? It could be, in the end, our ultimate competitive advantage. Without our encouragement as leaders, the customer tends to fall off the radar screen. Without our asking the provocative and respectfully encouraging questions of our people, the customer can even become a "hassle," or a "necessary evil" in our lives. In our zeal to bond with the people who report to us, we all too often commiserate and sympathize with their horror stories about how hard it is to please customers, how customers take advantage of us, why the phone ringing all day is such a problem for time management...and we agree, and by agreeing, we unknowingly plant the seeds that allow customers to be treated coldly, stupidly, and in a very unfriendly way. And this defeats the whole purpose of business! We're even willing to go farther: poor customer relations becomes the root cause of every business problem we have. Notice, if you will, how you are treated by the airlines that are having the biggest financial difficulties and how you are (almost always—no one's perfect, yet) treated by the people at Southwest Airlines, the only highly profitable airline. It is no accident that Southwest is the only airline that devotes all its thinking to the problems of the customer while the other airlines devote all of their thinking to the problems of the airline. The whole purpose of your business is to take such good care of the customer that the customer makes it a habit of returning to your business and buying more and more every time. But this will only happen when your people consciously build relationships with your customers. When they actively, consciously, creatively, cleverly, strategically, artfully, and gently build the relationship with the customer. Building the relationship does not come easy. It goes against our deepest habits. And it will never happen if your people see the customer as "a hassle...someone on the phone checking out prices...just an annoyance...someone interrupting me when I was just about to go to lunch...just a problem in my day...someone trying to return something...someone trying to challenge my years of expertise...some jerk...some idiot...." The reason this kind of disrespect and even contempt for the customer sinks into the psyche of our people is a lack of ongoing encouragement to think any other way. In other words, a lack of leadership. In other words, you and me. A bad attitude toward the customer always comes, in some subtle way, from the top. A fish rots from the head down. We as leaders set the tone. We either ask the right questions that start the ball rolling in our employees' minds, or we do not. If I am a leader, I want to ask questions that respect my people's intelligence. I want to treat them as if they are master psychologists, as if they are experts in customer behavior and customer thinking patterns—because they are. I want to ask how we can build more trust with the customer. I want to ask how we can convert a seemingly simple phone call into a warm relationship that leads to the customer liking us and wanting to buy from us no matter what the price is. I want to ask how we can get the sales force to win the customer's trust and repeat business. I want to ask for advice and help with the psychology of the customer. I want to ask the questions that will motivate my own managers to start thinking in terms of lifetime customers instead of single transactions. I might start a meeting with my team by saying, "Let's say you're a potential customer and you're calling my store. Let's say you're new in town and have no buying habits yet in this category of product. I'm the third store you have called. If I'm stressed and grumpy, and I simply give you the price you wanted for a product you're curious about and hang up, I may have lost you forever. What does that matter? A loss of a $69 won't kill us! "But consider the lifetime impact—or even just the next 10 years. What if that customer spends even just $400 a year in this category but has, because of this bad original call with us, formed a buying habit with a competitor? (Most people go to certain stores because it feels comfortable to go there.) In 10 years, that customer would have spent $4,000. That's $4,000 lost in less than a minute on a bad phone call. If someone lost $4,000 in one minute from the cash register, would they still be working for us?" Finally, in the end, I don't want to be too macho or too "professional" or too afraid of what people would think of me if I even used the word "friend" once in a while in my questions about how we can treat customers better. How would we treat that customer if that person were a dear friend? Why is the word friend so rarely heard in the world of business relations? Are friends really "better" than customers? Does your best friend regularly come by and give you money to help with the mortgage payment? Does your friend pull out his checkbook after having a beer with you and say, "Here's a little something for your daughter's dental bill"? No? Our customers do.

35

Best time for biggest challenges

It's so important to use your best time for your biggest challenge. Of course you can't always do this. Sometimes challenges have a way of blowing out their own hole in your timetable. But whenever possible, see if you can match up your prime biological (emotional, physical, mental) time with the big job or big communications you have to do. Many leaders are at their best in the first hours of the morning; others hit their prime in the late morning; others still, in the late afternoon. Whichever is your best time to shine, don't waste it on trivia and low-return activities. Invest that energy and peak attention into the big challenge you've been procrastinating about. Most of us confuse pleasure with happiness. We find great pleasure in spending our highest-energy state on small tasks, taking them out with relish and flair, blowing away all these minor, little must-do's with great bursts of energy and good cheer. But all the while, that big thing is lurking, waiting until we're tired and cranky to be fully contemplated, which is why it gets put off so often. Know ahead of time what your biggest challenge is. Set it up to be taken out with massive, unstoppable action while you are at your most resourceful and energetic. You do have a best time of day, mentally. Know when it is. Then use it! The ultimate source of a leader's professional happiness is the feeling of accomplishment you get when you take out the big thing! The look on your face alone will motivate others to follow you.

36

Use 10 Minute well

Man must not allow the clock and the calendar to blind him to the fact that each moment of his life is a miracle and a mystery. —H.G. Wells Contemporary philosopher William Irwin was asked what he thought the secret of effective leadership was. His answer was, “Learn to use 10 minutes intelligently. It will pay you huge dividends.” Often what separates a great leader from a lousy manager is just that: the ability to use 10 minutes well. The Irwin quote is one that we have on our office wall, reminding us that it really helps to have short, motivating quotations posted in plain view. It is a way to wake yourself up to your potential. Especially when you only have 10 minutes before your next appointment. Will you use it well? Or will you kill time? Our recent visit to a very successful leader’s office was enhanced by our noticing these words posted on the wall behind his desk—also a great guideline for using 10 minutes well: The Most Important Words in the English Language 5 most important words: I am proud of you! 4 most important words: What is your opinion? 3 most important words: If you please. 2 most important words: Thank you. 1 most important word: You. Here’s another quotation put up there on the office wall. This one’s from Charles Buxton, the famous lawyer and member of Parliament in the 1800s: “You will never ‘find’ time for anything, if you want time you must make it.” And sometimes that powerful leadership item we have not found time to do can be made to fit into the next 10- minute window.

37

Know what you want to grow

Most managers, especially those who struggle with "making plan," place the plan's numbers down around sixth on their daily priority list. Most struggling managers place these things above the "plan" in their priority hierarchy: 1. Not upsetting other people's feelings. 2. The commitment to looking extremely busy. 3. Fire-fighting and problem-solving. 4. Explaining and justifying other people's performances, both up and down the ladder. 5. Being liked. A few years ago we saw the brilliant business consultant Steve Hardison come into a struggling, financially failing company and turn everything around. He did it by altering priorities. The first thing he did was put HUGE whiteboards up all over the company meeting room to record and reflect daily sales numbers and activity. In the company's past, numbers had been an embarrassment. They were whispered about at the end of the month. If people weren't hitting good numbers, the management spent all its time listening to the reasons. The salespeople became good salespeople, but what they were learning to sell was their excuses, not their product. All management meetings focused on "Circumstances, Issues, and Situations that Prevent Us from Succeeding." The other day, we spoke to an operations manager at a company that was falling far short of its business projections. "We're not making plan," he said. "Why not?" "The economy. The weather. The war. The way kids are brought up today. The lack of good candidates for positions here. Company dysfunction. Industry decline. Government regulations. Competition moving in. No budget for sales training." "Other than that, what's in your way?" As we sat in on their company meetings, we observed that all the management meetings were about those subjects. All their meetings focused on the obstacles to success. What you focus on grows. Focus on numbers, and they, too, will grow. Huge.

38

Soften Your Thought

He is only advancing in life whose heart is getting softer, his blood warmer, his brain quicker, and his spirit entering into living peace. —John Ruskin, Art and Social Critic People who really succeed in leadership and in sales transform the entire activity away from the concept of managing and selling (even though they have high respect for that) into the day-to-day concept of building relationships. They always think in terms of their relationship with the other person: How can I make it better? How can I serve her? How can I contribute to her life today? How can I show him a demonstration of my commitment? How can I make her happier? How can I make it easier for him to access this information?

There is a continual expansion of the friendly side of the relationship. A leader knows that communication solves almost all problems. Avoidance worsens all problems. No leadership agreement was ever made outside of a conversation. So have your conversations be vital. Have a lot of conversations today and make them warm and comfortable. Have them all lead you to your ultimate goal. Master teacher Lance Secretan has written 13 books on leadership, and sums up his findings this way: "Leadership is not so much about technique and methods as it is about opening the heart. Leadership is about inspiration— of oneself and of others. Great leadership is about human experiences, not processes. Leadership is not a formula or a program, it is a human activity that comes from the heart and considers the hearts of others."

39

Coach your people to complete

Nothing is so fatiguing as the eternal hanging on of an uncompleted task.
—William James, Psychologist/Philosopher

If your people become more and more burned out and fatigued, it's up to you to help them redirect a course of action that leads them to the completion of previous projects. Once, long ago, we went to hear Cheryl Richardson give a presentation to "Coach U" over in Phoenix, and it was the first time we went to one of her meetings. We didn't know her or anything about Coach U, but we settled in for the talk. Richardson stood up and said to all of us, "Can you come up with a list of the top 10 things that are incomplete, that need to get done in your life? Can you come up with that list?" Of course, everyone could. So we did. We all wrote 10 things down! And then she told us a story to illustrate how she coaches her clients. She said she had a massage therapist who came in to see her, and she said to him, "What's the issue?" And the client said, "I need more business." She said, "Okay, I want you to write down the top 10 unfinished things that you need to complete in your life." And the client wrote them down. Then she said, "Now, I want you to make a commitment that you will get those complete." And the massage therapist said, "Okay, but that's not why I'm here to see you. I'm here because I need more business." Cheryl Richardson said, "I know that. Get this done, and you'll get more business." And her coaching client said, "What? This doesn't have anything to do with getting more business." Cheryl explained, "Actually, everything that is incomplete in your life is what I call an energy drain. And that is stopping you from creating more business." "Well, that doesn't make any sense to me." Cheryl said, "I only do this for a living! I counsel lots of clients, who all have this same thing. Are you willing to try it? If not, let's forget this relationship." "Well, okay, I guess, yeah. I need to get those things done anyway." So he made a commitment to get three of the 10 done by the next meeting. The following week, he reported back in and said, "I completed my assignment." And Cheryl asked, "What happened?" "Amazing! Even before the first week was over, three new people have called me out of the blue, and filled up my calendar." And Cheryl says, "That's how it works." We never forgot that lesson, and have re-taught it ever since. It's not just that your people have got all those incompletes out there, but the underlying thought of it, the subconscious knowledge is the energy drain. It's draining their productivity, imagination, and vitality away. Help them clean up those incompletes and their motivation will surprise you.

40

Do the math on your approach

We make a living by what we get, but we make a life by what we give. —Winston Churchill You will really enjoy motivating others if you start thinking of your life as a mathematical equation. We first saw the fun and benefit of this when our good friend and company CEO Duane Black solved the equation on two flip charts in front of a grateful gathering of managers. Here it is: When you are positive (picturing the math sign: +), you add something to any conversation or meeting you are part of. That's what being positive does, it adds. When you are negative (–), you subtract something from the conversation, the meeting, or the relationship you are part of. If you are negative enough times, you subtract so much from the relationship that there is no more relationship left. It's simple math. It's the law of the universe up there on the flip chart of life: positive adds, negative subtracts. As in math, when you add a negative, it diminishes the total. Add a negative person to the team, and the morale and spirit (and, therefore, productivity and profit) of the team is diminished. When you are a positive leader with positive thoughts about the future and the people you lead, you add something to every person you talk to. You bring something of value to every communication. Even every e-mail and voice mail (that's positive) adds something to the life of the person who receives it. Because positive (+) always adds something. It's a definite plus. It even runs deeper than that. If you think positive thoughts throughout the day, you are adding to your own deep inner experience of living. You are bringing a plus to your own spirit and energy with each positive thought. Your negative thoughts take away from the experience of being alive. They rob you of your energy. Say this to yourself: "I like this math. I like its simplicity. I can now do this math throughout my day. When I am experiencing negative thoughts about my team or my to-do list, I know it's time to take a break and regroup and refresh. It's time to call a time-out, close my eyes, and relax into my purpose and my mission. It's time to slow down and breathe into it. I take a lot of quick breaks like that during the day, and this practice is changing my life for the better. It is making me stronger and more energetic than ever before." Your own strength and energy motivates others. Or, as Carlos Castaneda said, "We either make ourselves miserable, or we make ourselves strong. The amount of work is the same."

41

Count Yourself

To decide to be at the level of choice, is to take responsibility for your life and to be in control of your life. —Arbie M. Dale, Psychologist/Author Leaders who take ownership motivate more effectively than leaders who pass themselves off as victims of the "corporate" structure or "upper management." That's because they have made a conscious decision to live at the level of choice. Throughout their day, their people hear them talk of "buying in." They are always heard saying, "Count me in. I'm in on that." The reason leaders living at the level of choice say, "Count me in," is not because they're apple-polishing, bootlicking "company" people. As a matter of fact, they don't much care who their company is! They're going to play full out for the company because it makes life more interesting, it makes work a better experience, and it's more fun. Whether it's a volleyball game on a picnic or the company's latest big project, it is more fun to buy in and play hard. Let's say the company orders everyone to break up into experimental teams. The manager with the victim's mind may say, "I'll wait and see if this is a good idea. Why are they throwing new stuff at us now? It's not enough that I have to work for a living; I've got to play all these games. What's this woo-woo, touchy-feely team stuff? I'm not going to buy into it yet; I'll wait and see. I'll give it five months." Meanwhile the owner-leader is saying, "Hey, I'm not going to judge this thing. That's a waste of mental energy. I'm buying in. Why? Because it deserves to be bought in to? No. I don't care if it deserves to be bought in to. I am buying in because it gives me more energy, it makes working more fun, I deserve to be happy at work, and I know from experience that buying into things works." True leadership inspires a spirit of buy-in. It's a spirit that has no relationship to whether the company "deserves" being bought in to—no relationship at all. The source of the buy-in is a personal commitment to have a great experience of life. That's where it comes from. It doesn't come from whether the company has "earned it." True leaders don't negatively personalize their companies. That habit is a form of mental illness. You stand for mental health. And when other people see that spirit in you, they are motivated to live by positive example too. They can see that it works. In sports, it's sometimes easier to see the value of this spirit. It seems obviously smart for an athlete to say, "I don't care if I'm playing for a minor league team or a major league team, it's in my self-interest to play full-out when I play." In companies, though, that would be a rare position to take. But true leaders are rare. They don't wait for the company to catch up to their lead. They take the lead. They don't wait for the company to give them something good to follow. No company will ever catch up with a great individual. A great individual will always be more creative than the company as a whole. Martin Luther King Jr. said, "Even if a man is called to be a street sweeper, he should sweep streets as Michelangelo painted or Beethoven composed music or Shakespeare wrote poetry."

42

Motivate Your People, First Just Relax

A frightened captain makes a frightened crew. —Lister Sinclair, Playwright/ Broadcaster The great music teacher and motivator of artists Rodney Mercado had a simple recipe for success. He said, "There are only two principles that you need to get to play great music or to live a great life: concentration and relaxation. And that's it. That is it." Scott recalls this remark and what he said back to Professor Mercado: "What? That doesn't have anything to do with music!""It has everything to do with music." And the way he taught relaxation was to say, "You need to have the maximum relaxation. For instance, if you want to play faster, Scott, you need to relax more. If you want to play louder, you need to relax more. If you want more sound coming out, you need to relax more." Up to this point in my life, it sounded like someone saying, "Well, if you want to become a cowboy, go to Harvard." It didn't make any sense. It seemed like a contradiction. Doesn't it sound like a contradiction? If you're going to be louder, stronger, and motivate people, don't you want to get them all hyped up and worked up? That's what I had always thought: light a fire! Get the lead out of your pants! So up to this point in my life, if I wanted to play faster, I would get hyped and tense up. And I would try harder. In any aspect of my life where I was trying to get more of something, I would become more tense from trying. But Mercado said, "I'm going to play a passage of music and I want you to just listen for a moment." I did. I don't remember the passage played at the time, but he almost ripped the strings off the violin. It was a virtuoso passage, but it sounded like he was going to make the strings just fly apart, there was so much sound and motion being produced. And I was awed. "Now, Scott, I want you to put your arm on top of my forearm while I play this passage, and feel what's going on while I'm doing this." When I put my arm on top of his forearm and he played this passage (and by the way, I'm trying to hang on for dear life, because his arm was flying), I was stunned, because his arm was almost totally relaxed. There was no tension in the muscles! And all of a sudden, I got it. Getting it changed my entire concept of playing the violin, but it also changed my concept of what I was doing in life. I had been tensing and straining for success instead of relaxing for it. The same formula works for a sprinter in track and field. What most sprinters do when they try to run faster is to put more effort into it. And they don't realize it but they tense up their muscles and their times actually drop. Trying harder slows them down! The sprinters don't realize that they're at their peak state of relaxation during their fastest times. I saw this firsthand while on the Brigham Young University track team when I was in a physical education class. I thought I was pretty tough stuff, so I raced one guy who wasn't on the track team. The guy barely beat me, but he was straining and out of control, and he just stumbled over the finish line. Then I met another guy who was one of the top sprinters on the BYU track team, and I challenged him to a race. We took off and he beat me by a wide margin. But there he was—Mercado's theory in motion—totally relaxed, totally fluid, and he just flew by me. So that principle is something that I have now adopted anytime I'm doing anything. If I'm in front of a jury, or my company, or any other group while I'm speaking, I know that the secret is relaxation, counterintuitive as that may seem.

Because what do most people do? They get nervous, they get tense, and their performance drops. But because of the training Mercado gave me, anytime I feel any tension at all, I slow down and relax all the more. His words always come back to me: "If you start shaking, there's only one way you can shake. You have to be tense. If you relax, you cannot shake. If you start shaking, that's a sign that you're not relaxing." Many team leaders get up in front of their teams or their company and are so nervous about speaking that they lose all ability to motivate anyone! We have attended countless conventions and retreats where the CEO totally blows an opportunity to motivate his people by stepping up to the podium and reading nervously from a script, or making a brief and tense talk that leaves everyone flat. A vice president of a large bank said to us of his CEO after the CEO had addressed 200 senior managers at a yearly conference: "Did you hear him? Did you see him? I mean, we wait all year to hear his words to us and he gives this nervous, brief, memorized talk! Like he couldn't be bothered to really talk to us!" "He was obviously nervous about his talk." "That's my point! To him, it was something he had to do. He obviously didn't want to do it. So his whole focus was on himself and what little he could get away with doing." "What do you want? He's not a public speaker." "Well, if he's going to lead a large company and ask us to hit the goals he's asking us to, he darn well better learn to be a public speaker! Because it's not about him, it's about us. We deserve better. We deserve someone talking to us, and I mean really talking to us. From the heart. Loud and strong and with passion and without a darn script!" "So, how do you really feel about his talk?" "That he came across as a pathetic little ball of ego who doesn't deserve to lead this company because he refuses to put himself on the line. We would have been more motivated if he had called in sick." If you're in a situation where you have to give a talk to your people and you feel tense, like it's not coming from the heart, practice relaxing on the spot. If your legs start to shake, don't worry. It's just feedback time, and the feedback from your body is that you're not relaxed. If you're relaxed, you cannot shake; it's physically impossible. Once you relax, you become a much better speaker. So don't just practice the talk you're going to give. Practice relaxing, too.

43

Don't through the quit switch

Most people succeed because they are determined to. People of mediocre ability sometimes achieve outstanding success because they don't know when to quit. —George Allen, Football Coach Every Olympic athlete, every leader, and every human being has a certain little-known brain part in common: a Quit Switch. Some people, out of lifelong habit, throw the Quit Switch at the first sign of frustration. Their workout gets difficult, so they throw the switch and go home. Their day of phone calls gets frustrating, so they throw the switch and go for coffee with a coworker for two hours of sympathetic negativity. Everyone has a Quit Switch. Not everyone knows it. Get to know it. Notice yourself flipping the switch. You can't quit and you won't quit until you throw the switch. A human being is built like any animal to persist until a goal is reached. Watch children get what they want and you'll see the natural, built-in persistence. Somewhere along the way, though, we learn about this little switch. Soon, we start flipping the switch. Some of us begin by flipping it after a severe frustration, and then start flipping it after medium frustrations, and until finally it is thrown in the face of any discomfort at all. We quit. If you weren't in the habit of throwing the switch too early, you would achieve virtually any goal you ever set. You would never give up on your team. You'd make every month's sales goal. You'd even lose all the weight you ever wanted to lose. You would achieve anything you wanted because you would not throw the switch. The Quit Switch is something you can focus on, learn about, and make work for you instead of against you. Whether you flip it early or late is only habit. The switchflipping habit is misinterpreted as lack of willpower, courage, drive, or desire, but that's nonsense. It's a habit. And like any habit, it can be replaced with another habit. Make it your habit not to throw the Quit Switch early in any process. Do not quit on yourself as a leader or on your team as producers. The less of a quitter you are, the more of a motivator you become.

44

Lead with enthusiasm

Nothing great was ever achieved without enthusiasm. —Ralph Waldo Emerson All the world's a stage. You are a great actor on that stage. So, when it is your turn to appear in a scene, be enthusiastic! Especially if you have something about which you need to fire up your team. If you have something to convince them of, try being really enthusiastic about what you have to say, simply as a place to come from. When your employee speaks in return, be enthusiastic. Glow. Sparkle. Radiate leadership and solutions. Pump yourself up. Take it to an even higher level. When you're ready to get the team involved, don't fade out—remember you are acting enthusiastic. You are an actor, and a good one. Finish strong. Enthusiasm is contagious. People love to be around it. It makes them smile and shake their heads; it can even make them laugh with pleasure at the dynamo that is you. Most managers make the mistake of not doing this. They act reserved, cool, and "professional." They don't act "professional" because they are professional; they do it because they're scared (about how they're coming across), and they think if they act cool they will be safe. We spoke with Jeremy about a talk we had him give to his team. "You seemed a little less than enthusiastic about this new commission system, Jeremy."

"Really? I didn't realize that." "That's the point." "What do you mean?" Jeremy asked. "You aren't realizing your lack of enthusiasm in front of your team because you are choosing not to be conscious of it." "How is it a choice?" "You are choosing to be less than enthusiastic." "Oh, I don't think so. It doesn't feel like I'm making any kind of choice." Jeremy said. "You speak Spanish, don't you Jeremy?" "Yes, I do. I'm bilingual. It helps with certain customers." "Did you realize that you gave your talk to your team in English? Were you aware of that?" "Yes, of course." "Did you choose that?" "Of course I chose it! The team all speaks English. What are you driving at here?" Jeremy asked. "Your choice to speak in English was as clear and definite a choice as your choice to be unenthusiastic. You have an equally clear choice about enthusiasm (or no enthusiasm) as you do about choosing between English and Spanish. We recommend you stop choosing to be unenthusiastic with your people." Jeremy said nothing. "Because being calm and professional doesn't motivate. A chilly demeanor doesn't make much of an impression. It is immediately forgotten, along with the idea you are promoting." Enthusiasm comes from the Greek words en theos, which translate to "the God within," the most spirited and spiritual you. You times 10. Like the you when you were a little kid riding your bike with no hands. Enthusiasm is contagious. If you are excited about your idea, everyone else will be excited. That's how it works. Always remember Emerson's observation, "Nothing great was ever achieved without enthusiasm." You can lead with enthusiasm, or you can lead without enthusiasm. Those are your choices. One choice leads to a highly motivated team; the other leads to long-term problems. "But how can I be enthusiastic when I'm not?" Jeremy finally said. We have managers ask that question all the time. The answer is easy. The way to be enthusiastic is to act enthusiastic. There isn't a person in the world who can tell the difference if you put your heart and soul into your acting. And about a minute and a half into your acting, the funniest thing starts to happen: the enthusiasm becomes real. You do feel it. And so does your team.

45

Encourage your people to concentration

The first law of success is concentration, to bend all the energies to one point, and to go directly to that point, looking neither to the right, nor to the left. —William Matthews, Journalist

The other principle that Professor Mercado believed in was concentration, or focus. And to drive it home to his students, he had a bizarre system. Scott recalls: Professor Mercado had us play music recitals, as most teachers do. But at these recitals, he would have us play our pieces twice. The first time we would play them like at any standard recital. We would all play "Mary Had A Little Lamb" on the violin and the audience would politely clap. And then, after that performance was done and everybody had a chance to play the traditional way, Mercado would say, "Okay, now we're going to play it again. Everyone's going to have a chance to perform their piece again." But this time, while the performers were performing, Mercado would pass out slips of paper to the audience. The slips would have instructions written on them, such as, "Go up to the performer and tickle his ear." "Sing 'Yankee Doodle Dandy.'" Mercado would even say to the performer's accompanist, "Speed up." "Slow down." "Stop." Mercado would then physically come up to us while we were playing and he would do things even more radical than that! He would take our bow away. He would untune our strings so you couldn't get any sound out of the string. Then, he would start tuning the instrument back up. Basically, all hell would break loose during these second performances. And when it was over, he would ask each one of us, "Which performance was better? The first, normal one, or the second one, where all hell was breaking loose?" When I ask people nowadays what they think the answer was, most people guess it was the first, normal way. But invariably, the second performance was better. The one in which we were most distracted! And we all admitted that. And then he would ask us the question, "Why?"

And the answer was pretty obvious to the musicians who had lived through it, and that was because we were "forced" to totally concentrate and focus on our music internally. We had been compelled to exclude every other environmental impact or influence and just wipe it out. If we had paid any attention to what was going on around us, we would have become hopelessly lost. And so by that total internal focus on what we were attempting to produce—the music—and excluding everything else, including our accompanist, we performed fantastically in the face of extraordinary odds. You can't imagine anything that difficult. The lesson was huge. And I use the lesson this way: the next time I'm upset by the chaos and problems swirling all around me, I use it to focus myself even more. If you want your people to be truly inspired by your example, show them how to use distractions to focus them even more, not less. Show them how it's done. The great Igor Stravinsky once said, "My freedom will be so much the greater and more meaningful the more narrowly I limit my field of action and the more I surround myself with obstacles. Whatever diminishes constraint diminishes strength. The more constraints one imposes, the more one frees one's self of the chains that shackle the spirit."

46

Inspire Inner Stability

Becoming a leader is synonymous with becoming yourself. It is precisely that simple, and it is also that difficult. —Warren Bennis

People look so hard for stability. All the leaders we coach and work with on some level or another are secretly trying to find more stability in their work, in their careers, and especially in their companies. But the key to stability is not to look outside yourself for it. It's useless to try to find it from your company or from your industry. It only works to look inside. You need to turn the mirror around so you can see yourself. You need to find it inside your own enthusiasm for work. And sometimes that inner enthusiasm must be built from scratch, from improvisation. Psychologist Nathaniel Branden puts it this way: "Chances are, when you were young, you were told, in effect, 'Listen, kid, here is the news: life is not about you. Life is not about what you want. What you want is not important. Life is about doing what others expect of you.' If you accepted this idea, later on you wondered what had happened to your fire. Where had your enthusiasm for living gone?" Ask yourself the following questions: Do I feel good about myself at the end of the day? Am I proud of my leadership today? Do I feel that wonderful, little feeling that I get when we've had a good day and we feel like we've really nailed it? If so, that opinion is vital (and visible) to the people I want to motivate. If you can consciously build that level of confidence in yourself as a leader, then you can put stability into your career. That's where real stability comes from, especially in this era of rapid-fire external changes. The marketplace changes, each industry changes, the whole world changes. Every morning as we open up the newspaper or turn on the news, something radical is different. Something important will never be the same.

This rapid change is terrifying to unstable people. Unstable people wish things would just stay the same. Even if the company comes up with a new compensation plan, new pricing for customers, new ways of hiring, or anything that might look like future stability, I still can't go to sleep. Change happens. Does anything motivate people more than to be in the presence of a leader with inner stability and self-esteem? We build self-esteem in small increments just like athletes build strength. They don't do it overnight. They do it day by day, adding a little more weight to the bar, adding a little more distance to the run. Pretty soon, they are magnificent, powerful, wonderful athletes. The same is true with leadership; it happens the same way. A little bit every day—a little better at communication, a little better at delegation, a little better at servant leadership, a little bit better at listening to people and executing plans. Getting 2 percent, maybe 4 percent, better. No more than that. But it's conscious and it is inspiring to be around.

47

Being Right

I must follow the people. Am I not their leader? —Benjamin Disraeli When people are promoted to a management position, they often feel that it's very important that everybody sees that they know what they're doing.

So they twist that into a drive to be right. They think people will only admire them if they're right about things, and by doing this, they make it really hard for themselves to be human with their people. They make it hard for themselves to admit that they're wrong and to say to other people, "You know what? You're right about that." A really strong, motivational leader who is admired and respected is one who does not have to be right about anything. Ever. It is much more powerful to say to someone, "You know, now that I've listened to you, one thing I've realized is that you are right about that. And I'm going to take some steps to get that done." That's a person who will eventually motivate others. Because being right is never going to matter in the long run. What's going to matter in the long run is achieving something. I can be wrong about absolutely everything day in, day out, and still be a wonderfully great leader. Why? Because I brought out the best in my people. I've taught them to make their own decisions. I have drawn out their strengths, their loyalties, their high performance, and all the numbers have tumbled in my direction.

48

Wake Yourself Up

Too many people are thinking of security instead of opportunity. They seem to be more afraid of life than death. —James F. Bymes, former Secretary of State Change will scare my people to the degree that it scares me.

So another way to consciously build my inner strength as a leader is to increase my awareness of what life is like, what the world is like, and what the business community is like. As I become more aware of that, I become a better leader. I don't want to just put my head into the sand, and say, "But we've been doing it this way for 20 years." I don't want to always be heard saying, "I don't want to think about it, I don't want to be aware that anything's changed. I just want everything to be like it used to be; I want people to be the way they used to be." But if I don't want to have a real understanding of what people are like today, especially younger people, and how they're perceiving life, my leadership skills will decline over the years, and pretty soon I'll become almost irrelevant. As Nathaniel Branden writes in Self-Esteem at Work: We now live in a global economy characterized by rapid change, accelerating scientific and technological breakthroughs, and an unprecedented level of competitiveness. These developments create demands for higher levels of education and training than were required from previous generations. ... What is not understood is that these developments also create new demands on our psychological resources. Specifically, these developments ask for greater capacity for innovation, number one, self-management, number two, personal responsibility, number three, and self-direction. It used to be that leaders were led by other leaders, managers were managed by other managers, and there wasn't that much wiggle room in between. We were told what to do, then we told other people what to do, and it was basically a hierarchical, military-type system.

A topdown silo. But now, things are so complex and ever-changing— it's like calling audible plays at the line of scrimmage every single time, instead of running regular plays. That's what global business life is like right now. Life has changed profoundly. And it will continue to change even faster as time goes on. That's good news for a leader committed to being more and more awake to it.

49

Always show them

I hear and I forget. I see and I remember. I do and I understand. —Confucius

A lot of great sports players go into coaching, but it just doesn't quite work. Sometimes, it turns out, they're just not very good at it. And there's a reason. It's not mysterious. They are simply not totally conscious of what it was that made them great players. A lot of what they did as players was intuitive and subconscious. It was the feel of the thing. And so they have a very hard time teaching it to others and communicating it because they didn't even know what it was. The best batting coach of all time was Charlie Lau. He taught a baseball player by the name of George Brett how to hit. And, as you may know, George Brett was one of the greatest hitters of all time, hitting in the high . 300s all the time. But Charlie Lau—his coach, his instructor, his teacher—had a lifetime batting average of .255! Charlie Lau was a mediocre hitter at best. But because Lau had to struggle so hard just to stay in the majors, just to keep his job, he learned hitting inside and out. He became extremely conscious of how it was done. Therefore, he was great at teaching it. So when you figure something out, anything, that your people are not doing up to the level that you'd like them to be doing, show them what to do. Take the bat in your own hands and show them how to hit. Christina wanted our opinion of a problem she was having with her team. "My people aren't great with customers," Christina said. "I believe they leave a lot of business on the table." "Tell us how you'd like your people to be different." "Well, here's what I think," said Christina. "I bet if my people talked to customers a little differently, asked them more questions, got more interested in their lives, that they'd find out a few other areas in which they could help them out. They'd find out areas where we might have a product or a service that would help the customer. Instead, my people just sell people things, they're just ordertakers, and our sales aren't as high as they could be if my team took a greater interest in the customer." "What have you done about that?" "First, I sent that opinion around in an e-mail, and that didn't go over very well," said Christina. "Of course it wouldn't." "Right," she said. "Then I called some of my managers and said, 'I want you to get your people to do more of this!'"

"Did that go well?" "No." "What else did you do?" "I called HR," said Christina. "I told HR we really needed training in this. Relationships. The upsell." "How did the training go?" "Still waiting," said Christina. "I'm still waiting for an answer to my request for it." "Christina, do this yourself! A true leader, a really powerful leader, who's consciously motivating others to great performance, will show them how to do it. A true leader will figure out what it is that she wants her people to do and then will go in and demonstrate it." We watched Christina later as she talked to her team. "Here, let me work with you today," she told them. "I want to talk to customers who come in. All I'd like you to do is be with me and watch me do it, be there, help out, ask questions if you can think of them. But let me do the work." Christina learned to show people the way she wished they would do it. She realized that the best way to communicate that was to do it herself. That was her new leverage point, and by doing it that way her people got excited and understood quickly. If you just tell your people, "I want you to do more of that, you've got to get better at that," it falls on deaf ears, and sometimes even worse. Sometimes it causes people to defend how they're doing it. Or it causes people to tell you, "I don't have time to do that." To really motivate, talk less and demonstrate more.

50
Focus like a camera

Most of the successful people I've known are the ones who do more listening than talking. —Bernard Baruch

We want to introduce a kind of leadership that we find in only one out of every 10 leaders we work with. We call it focused leadership. It's the ability on the part of a leader to be absolutely focused. And what we mean by focused is not hard-core, intense concentration, as if you're forcing something. It's really the opposite. It's a much more relaxed sense of focus. So what we'd like you to do is picture a camera focusing: you're looking through the camera and it looks fuzzy, and as you turn the focus dial or knob, you don't have to jam it or whack it or slam it. All you have to do is move it very gently one way or the other, and, all of a sudden, the whole picture comes into focus. That same thing can happen with your outlook as a leader. Someone will walk into your office and sit down. Notice that you are beginning to focus on him like a camera, because there's that internal dial in you that is very slowly moving until the person across the way comes into a gentle, relaxed, absolute focus. And now, you may breathe a sigh (go ahead), and take a deep breath, and say, "Tell me what's on your mind. How're you doing? Let's talk about this issue here." Your employee will pick up on this gentle, relaxed sense of focus, and be honored by it. They will be thinking this about you: It's as if we're the only two people in the world right now. It feels like we're on a desert island and we've got all the time in the world. You will be thinking, And I'm listening to you, and you and I are going to get to the bottom of this. But not in a rushed way, and not because we have to. But because that's where the conversation will take us in an open way. In a way that honors you and acknowledges you, and hears you, and we just talk. We're going to exchange some ideas, I'm going to ask you some questions, and we're going to find out what the two of us think about this. I'm not going to tell you what to do. And I'm not someone who's got an agenda that's hidden that I'm going to reveal to you bit by bit as I talk to you. I'm wide open. I'm like a camera. And you are a great leader. You already know the other kind of leader, the not so great one; the leader who comes into meetings carrying his electronic organizer, and while he's sitting in the meeting, he'll be returning e-mails, picking up his vibrating cell phone every two or three minutes to see who it is, and also trying to be in the meeting. He's thinking he's multitasking, but really, he's just not focused. And everyone who runs into that leader feels diminished by the exchange. We talked to Richie about a leader of his who behaves that way. "I always feel about him that he's someone who has no time for me," Richie said. "That's someone who'd really rather not be talking to me right now. The minute I sit down he rattles off a list of ideas he has. He doesn't care what I think."

That "leader" doesn't know that of the hundred people he communicated with that week in some form—some by e-mail, some by PDA, some by fax, some by phone, some in person, some in the hallway—all 100 people have been distanced by this behavior. And maybe, deep down, this dysfunctional manager senses the distancing that's happening. And so he has an uneasy feeling. He must fix this sense of things not going right. But rather than slowing down, he speeds up even more! Once we told a manager who behaved this way that he ought to wear a sign around his neck. "What do you mean a sign around my neck?" "You ought to wear a sign, like people do in treatment centers when they're trying to solve a personal issue, and the sign should say, 'I HAVE NO TIME FOR YOU.'" He said nothing. "You also might want to have your e-mail send an automatic reply to people saying, 'I HAVE NO TIME FOR YOU.'" "Why would I do that? I could never do that," he said. "You're doing it now. You're sending that message now. This way, you'd just be more up front about it." When we coach managers to open up and focus on their people, like a camera, it actually saves them time in the long run. Because it takes a lot less time to manage a motivated, trusting team than it does to work with a demoralized, upset team.

51

Think of management as easy

Always think of what you have to do as easy and it will be. —Émile Coué, Psychologist A thought is more than a thought, it creates your reality. The role of thought in managing people and results cannot be overestimated. What you think about how hard your work is more important than any so-called interpreted "reality" about your work. If you think motivating people is hard, it is hard. There's no difference. As Shakespeare said, "There is nothing bad nor good, but thinking makes it so." If you think it's hard and uncomfortable to get on the telephone, then it is. If you think you're happy and relaxed picking up the phone, then you are. It's important to see the power that thought has in the world of leadership. If you're thinking thoughts that bring you down, you're not going to have a very good "people" day. Leadership requires high levels of humanity. To be great leaders, we need to share our humanity and receive our people's humanity all day. You can be a leader who is successful at motivating others. Thought is the key. When Napoleon Hill wrote Think and Grow Rich (Ballantine Books, Reissue Ed., 1990) his point was that you can think yourself into a perfect position to become successful. Many people have followed his instructions and done it. We can also do it. Is it easy? Actually it can be. For as the great and celebrated psychologist Coué said, "Always think of what you have to do as easy and it will be." One thing's for sure: It can't be harder than you think it is.

52

Cultivate the power of Reassurance

In organizations, real power and energy is generated through relationships. The patterns of relationships and the capacities to form them are more important than tasks, functions, roles, and positions. —Margaret Wheatly, Management Consultant One of the most valuable additions to a person's life that a leader can provide is reassurance. You won't hear about it in any management seminars, and that's a shame, because there's nothing more motivating than a healthy dose of reassurance. How many leadership books focus on it? None. How important is it as a management tool? It's the most important tool. How many times during the day do you ask yourself, "How reassuring was I in that conversation?" How many times before a conversation do you ask yourself, "Now, how can I be really reassuring to this person, so that they leave reassured that everything's going to be all right, and that they've got the skills to do this job?" If you integrate reassurance into your personal system and managerial approach, things will change on your team. The state of mind of your people will be altered for the better.

People look to their leaders for reassurance. Period. Truth is, they don't get that reassurance most of the time. They get the opposite. They get the impression that the team is racing and behind the gun. Their manager's demeanor and language cries out, "We've got to go, go, go. I'm late, I'm sorry I'm late for my meeting with you." "I'm on the phone and it's rush, rush, and we're behind the eight ball, and it's crazy around here." The problem with that message is that it's not reassuring. When you do the chaos act and convey a crisis mentality, it undermines productivity. The last thing you wanted. The concept that counters all of that and cures it forever is the concept of reassurance. Once you'got the concept, make it a practice. Watch the results.

53

Phase out Disagreement

The best way to have a good idea is to have lots of ideas. —Linus Pauling, Nobel Prize–Scientist When you listen to another person during a meeting or in a one-on-one, one of the best things you can do is to stop disagreeing. In other words, listen for the value in what someone has to say; don't listen for whether you agree with them, because every time you disagree with one of your employees, you throw them off balance and put them in a worse mood than they were before.

If I disagree with you, what will you do? You will defend yourself. Won't you? All humans do. And you are human. So you go on the defensive. You don't just say, "Oh, okay, yeah, I see your point of view. Yes sir, you're right, and I was wrong, and so that's good. I'm in a better mood now. What else do you disagree with?" That won't happen. If you're going to disagree with someone, accept the consequences. The main consequence: you've lowered that person's mood. And the consequence of putting someone in a low mood? That person's not going to do a very motivated job. People do not do well when they're in a low mood. Their energy goes away. However, if you were to start listening for the value in what people had to say, instead of whether you disagreed with them, their moods would still be good as you talked. In fact, by listening for the value in everyone in the team meeting instead of listening for whether you agree, the mood of the whole room will rise. You can influence an entire team meeting by having it be your personal policy as a leader to always listen for the value in what someone has to say. Most managers don't do that. Most managers let someone talk, and then say, "No, that's not right. I don't agree with that." Then they wonder why their employees now feel undervalued. But it was the manager's obsession with disagreement that made the employee feel undervalued. How does making someone feel stupid make someone ready to be more motivated? Does anyone ever think, “Okay, you’ve made me feel stupid, I’m really ready to work hard now. I’m feelin’ stupid, let’s go!”

Most managers tell us, “Well, if I disagree, I disagree. All I’m doing is disagreeing.” Okay, but every time you disagree, you’re going to challenge somebody and make them feel stupid, and that’s the consequence. Sometimes you have to disagree. But the less you do, the better the team will be for you. The more motivated your people will be.

54

Keep learning

Leaders grow; they are not made. —Peter F. Drucker Stay on your learning curve. And let your people see you learning. Don't show them a "know-it-all" attitude all the time. Let them know that you are a work in progress. That will make it easier for them to approach you with good ideas. Most managers are so insecure in their role that they continuously try to look like they know more than everyone else. They never go to seminars. They scorn the latest book on management theory. But this attitude is actually demoralizing to their followers. We all can learn something new about our profession every day. Little by little, we can add to our knowledge base, and that increases our professional strength and capacity to help others.

The great leaders are like the best conductors—they reach beyond the notes to reach the magic in the players. —Blaine Lee, Management Consultant Managers make a big mistake when they get bossy. It is a sure sign of insecurity when you push the point that you're the boss. You can be decisive and courageous, and hold people accountable without ever being pushy and bossy about it. Dee Hock, founder and CEO emeritus of VISA International, put it this way: "Control is not leadership; management is not leadership; leadership is leadership is leadership. If you seek to lead, invest at least 50 percent of your time leading yourself—your own purpose, ethics, principles, motivation, conduct. Invest at least 20 percent leading those with authority over you and 15 percent leading your peers. If you don't understand that you work for your mislabeled 'subordinates,' then you know nothing of leadership. You know only tyranny." Those are strong words for the bossy. But the bossy are clueless about human nature, especially in these times. All of our people are thinkers. They aren't just robots. The old style of militaristic leadership is no longer appropriate. It's no longer leadership. Today's leaders find the magic in their players.

I have more fun, and enjoy more financial success, when I stop trying to get what I want and start helping other people get what they want. —Spencer Johnson, Business Author How would we know what kind of a leader you are? There is one very fast way: We would ask the people who follow you. They know. And what they say is true. You are who they say you are. So listen to them! Understand them. People are highly motivated by listeners, listeners like you "who get" what their problems are. Always be mindful. In the words of Thich Nhat Hanh: When we are mindful, we notice that another person suffers. If one person suffers, that person needs to talk to someone in order to get relief. We have to offer our presence, and we have to listen deeply to the other person who is suffering. That is the practice of love—deep listening. But if we are full of anger, irritation, and prejudices, we don't have the capacity to listen deeply to the people we love. If people we love cannot communicate with us, then they will suffer more. Learning how to listen deeply is our responsibility. We are motivated by the desire to relieve suffering. That is why we listen. We need to listen with all our heart, without intention to judge, condemn, or criticize. And if we listen in that way for one hour, we are practicing true love. We don't have to say anything; we just need to listen. To help your people get what they want, be mindful of them and listen to them until you find out what they really want. Then, make their goals fit inside the team objectives. Show them the link. That's how long-lasting motivation finally happens.

55

Play it Lightly

The leadership instinct you are born with is the backbone. Then you develop the funny bone and the wishbone that go with it. —Elaine Agather, CEO, JPMorgan Bank The most motivated people we work with are not taking themselves all that seriously. The ones who struggle the most view the company's next success as their own mortgage payment or what holds their marriage together. The managers who are the most creative, productive, and innovative see business as a chess game, played for fun and challenge. They conceive of all kinds of lovely moves and counterstrategies. And when they "lose," they just set up the pieces again even more excitedly. The worst failures and most miserable people at work are the ones who take everything too seriously. They are grim, discouraged, and bitter. They use only 10 percent of their brains all day. Their brains, once so huge in childhood, are now hardened and contracted into resentment and worry. Here's what the overly serious people miss: the fun, the creativity, the lighthearted ideas, the intuition, the good spirits, the easy energy, and the quick laughter that brings people close to each other. They miss that. So no wonder they fail at what they're doing. Anytime we take something that seriously, we will find ways to subtly and subconsciously run away from it all day. Secretly, we are like children. We resist the serious. America's most respected scholar on organizational leadership today is Warren Bennis. In his book On Becoming a Leader, Revised Ed. (Perseus Publishing, 2003), he stresses the difference between a leader and a manager: "The leader innovates; the manager administrates. The leader focuses on people; the manager focuses on systems and structure. The leader inspires; the manager controls. The leader is his own person; the manager is a good soldier. The leader sees the long-term; the manager sees the short-term." G.K. Chesterton once said that angels can fly only because they take themselves lightly. We say the same of leaders.

56

Keep all your smallest promises

Great things are not done by impulse, but by a series of small things brought together. —Vincent van Gogh People are motivated by people they trust.

The trust of your people is not difficult to obtain. You can win it. And because it's so important to motivating them, you must win it. So you must never ever be late to your own meetings. Ever. Such a thing will destroy all trust you've built up with seven out of 10 people, because it means to them that you cannot be counted on to keep your word. We explained this to Jeff after working with his team for a while and noticing that he was not keeping any of his "small" promises. "Hey, it's no biggie!" Jeff would say. "I'm a little late, or I forget to get somebody a parking pass, so what? I'm a big-picture guy. I'm not all that anal." "It's your word, Jeff. If you can't keep it in the small things, no one will trust it in any of the big things." "Well," said Jeff, "what should I do? Become someone I'm not? Get a personality transplant? Get some good drugs that keep me focused?" "You must do everything you say you're going to do for your people, when you say you're going to do it. If you say you'll call tomorrow, you must. If you say you'll get them the documents by Friday, you must move heaven and earth to do that. It's everything. Trust is earned, not just by the big things, but even more so by the little things. Even more so."

57

Give Power to the person

When I'm getting ready to persuade a person, I spend one-third of the time thinking about myself, what I'm going to say, and twothirds of the time thinking about him and what he is going to say. —Abraham Lincoln When I'm in a leadership position, there's always a hidden fear inside the person I'm leading and about to talk to. If I don't understand that fear, I'm going to have a very hard time creating agreements with that person. And long-lasting motivation is all about creating agreements. My goal is to get my people to agree to work with me. I may want them to agree with me to perform at a higher level, or to get some work done that I think needs to be done, or to communicate with me differently, or to treat the customer differently. In all these cases, it's an agreement that I need. But there's a reason (you know what it is by now— here's a hint: it's fear) why the person on the other side will push back at me and try not to agree with me. And once we understand that reason, we have the ability to create agreements much faster. The focus of my understanding must always be: How do I remove the fear? Top hypnotists will tell you that they can't even begin to work with a subject whom they can't relax. When a person is not relaxed, they are not open to suggestion, hypnotic or otherwise.

Most managers who try to create agreements with other people actually cause the fear in the other person to get worse as the conversation goes on. So how do you create an agreement in such a way that the employee's fear buttons are not being pushed, and they're not pushing back in self-defense? By asking questions. Because questions honor the employee's thoughts and feelings. When people fear losing power and balance and push back (with objections, defensiveness, etc.), it looks like strength! It looks like, "Well, there's a feisty person! There's a person who knows his own mind. There's a person who's not going to get pushed around." Not true. That's a scared person! People don't want you to sell them on your idea, they want to sell themselves. They want it to be their idea to do the thing, not yours. That's the secret to motivation, right there. Let's say you want one of your employees to get forms turned back to you in a more timely manner. If you talk to that employee in an assertive way and say, "You know what, I need to talk to you. I didn't get those forms from you on time." You know what happens? Defensiveness and fear: "There's no way I could get them back to you on time because our computer system was down for two days. Actually, our people did pretty well given what was going on here at this office. We did very well, as a matter of fact, and we're doing better than can be expected down here." Your employee is defending what went on, because your employee is afraid that he will be judged poorly, that he might even be asked to leave the company because he can't get his forms in on time. And all you've done—the only mistake you have made—is you've put something aggressively out there that pushed his button, so you've awakened the fear, and caused him to push back. And if you are clueless about fear and don't know what is going on, you are liable to push even more buttons in response to the fear. You might say, "Well you know, that computer system was down at another division across town and they got theirs in on time." And now your employee is more frightened, even more anxious. "Yeah, but they've got a bigger staff than we do. We're understaffed here. Always have been." The more you push, the more he pushes back. The more offensive you are, the more defensive he is. And, the more defensive he is, the less likely he is to turn those forms in on time next week, which is all you wanted in the first place. It was all you wanted, but it was what you yourself made unlikely. This very human push–push back dynamic challenges marriages, it slows down careers, and it makes a manager's life miserable. What a manager can do is ask gentle questions and let the people they lead think and speak and make their own fresh commitments. That's how motivation happens.

58

Don't forget to Breath

In war, as in peace, a man needs all the brains he can get. Nobody ever had too many brains. Brains come from oxygen. Oxygen comes from the lungs where the air goes when we breathe. The oxygen in the air gets into the blood and travels to the brain. Any fool can double the size of his lungs. —George Patton

Scott Richardson recalls the role breathing plays in achieving success as a leader. Yes, breathing, as in, "Don't forget to breathe." Scott recalls: My first mentor and music coach, Rodney Mercado, never actually mentioned it. We never spoke about it, and yet I noticed it, and I copied him and modeled him. Because when Mercado played an instrument, he was taking some of the most extraordinarily deep breaths that I'd ever heard a human being take. And so even though he never mentioned it, I figured, if it works for him, I'm going to do the same thing. And since then, I've learned how important breath is to our energy, our focus, and our concentration. So, I would take a deep breath inward right before I started to play the violin, and then I would breathe out as I was bowing. And then as I changed the bow stroke, I would take another breath, and so I would breathe in unison with the music I was performing. I still do this to this day. Putting so much energy and intensity (Mercado's favorite word) into the performance was what produced the result that would move people who heard it. As leaders, our own energy and intensity are monitored by our people. They take many of their own subtle psychological cues from how we look—our movements and expressions (or lack of them). This is why we must learn to breathe deeply and lead. To really get out there and lead with enthusiasm. To generate excitement, and then breathe again, even more deeply. The word inspire literally means "to breathe in."

We don't want to stagnate all day breathing shallowly behind our desk or in front of our computer. That won't inspire anyone.

59

You got time

Start by doing what's necessary, then what's possible, and suddenly you are doing the impossible. —St. Francis Most managers do small things all day long. They start the day by doing all the easy things. They go through their e-mail over and over again. They ask themselves subconsciously: What are some little tasks that I can do that aren't difficult? What are things to do that will make it look like I'm being a manager while I figure out what really needs to be done? If anybody were watching me, would they say I am just doing what a manager needs to do? I'm doing what I need to do; these things need to be done sooner or later. But a motivational leader has the ability and the opportunity to live life differently, to take the time to live by rational choice of priority instead of feelings, to leave the infantile behind. The key is taking the time. And what works against this is the sense that time is getting away, there's really not enough time in the day. But you can learn to stay grounded in this fact: we all have 24 hours. It doesn't matter how rich or powerful you are, you still only have 24 hours—not a minute more.

The sun rises and sets for everyone the same way. And so there's no sense in saying, "I don't have as much time as other people. I'd love to do that but I don't have the time." That's just not true. Only you can slow your own sense of time down to the speed of life by choosing what you choose to do. And once you do, it becomes that much easier to motivate and teach others to do the same.

60

Use the deadlines

The best way to predict the future is to create it. —Peter F. Drucker Put your requests into a time frame. If there is no real time frame, make one up. If you want a report from someone, finish your request by asking, "And may I have this by the end of our business day Thursday?" Various dictionaries describe a deadline as a time by which something must be done; originally meaning "a line that does not move," and "a line around a military prison beyond which an escaping prisoner could be shot." Literally, it is a line over which the person or project becomes dead! Deadlines propel action. So when you want to get people into action, give them a deadline. If you make a request without including a date or time, then you don't have anything specific that you can check in on. You have a "wished for" and "hoped for"action hanging out there in space with no time involved. People are only motivated when we use both space and time. The space-time continuum is a motivator's best friend. Once, we were leisurely writing a book when the publisher called back to impose a month-away deadline to make the fall catalog for the big Christmas sales season. Then, all of a sudden, we swung into gear, writing and editing 10 hours a day, until we delivered the finished manuscript to our publisher. It turned out to be the bestwritten book we'd ever done. Without a deadline, there is no goal, just a nebulous request that adds to the general confusion at work. You will be doing a person a favor by putting your request into a time frame. And if the time is too short, he or she can negotiate it. Let your people participate. It isn't a matter of who gets to set the deadline, it's a matter of having one. Either way, it is settled, clear, and complete. Most managers don't do this. They have hundreds of unfulfilled requests floating around the workplace, because they aren't prioritized. Those requests keep getting put off. Don't they? Deadlines will fix all of that.

61

Translate worry into concern

Difficulties are meant to rouse, not discourage. —William Ellery Channing, Minister/Psychologist Leaders don't help anyone by worrying. Worry is a misuse of their imagination. Practice upgrading your worry to concern. Then, once you state your concern, create your action plan to address it. If we respond to our problems in life by worrying about them, we will reduce our mood and energy, and lower our self-esteem. Being a worrier is hardly a powerful self-concept. It also is not inspiring to others when they see their leader worrying. Instead of worrying, imagine some action you could take now, something bold and beautiful inspired by the current so-called "problem." Getting into that habit raises self-esteem and increases energy levels and concurrent love of life. People are more motivated by people in love with life than by people who worry about life.f you don't think about the future, you won't have one. —Henry Ford Managers who approach life as if they're still children, or as adults who are living out their unresolved childhood issues, will not be able to focus on their employees, their customers, or the hunt for great prosperity. Leadership requires that your logical, problem-solving left brain be in charge of your right brain. It requires a fierce intellect willing to hang in there against all your people's complaints (real and imaginary). It requires a thrill in finding a new route to solutions. Leadership requires that the chess master in you be in charge of the thinking and decision-making processes throughout the day. Leadership is about making clear, smart decisions about where and how you spend your time. Leading people is about getting smarter with your time every day. The great chess master Kasparov lived by his motto: "Think seven moves ahead." Intellectually, motivating others is about reverse engineering. You decide what you want, and then you think backwards from that. You begin at the end and engineer backwards to this fresh moment right now. Always have the end in mind when you approach your team or when you make that phone call. Those people best at motivating others are the ones who are the most conscious of what they're doing. They are the continuous thinkers, and their people appreciate them for it. As you drive around today, think things through. Think about what you would appreciate most if you were a member of your own team. Think about ways to connect and gain trust. Think. Think about that nice extra touch, that nice little piece of communication you want to make. Think about the questions you want to ask. Think like a brilliant detective. It's a crime that your employee is not performing at her full potential. It's a crime that she is considering leaving the company. Solve that crime.

62

Build a culture of acknowledgment

I have always said that if I were a rich man I'd hire a professional praiser. —Sir Osbert Sitwell, Poet One way to motivate others better is to change the question you ask yourself each day. Instead of, "How do I get them to do less of what bothers me," I might want to change that to, "What is the best thing I can do to get my team to do more of what I want them to do?" Most managers find out what's wrong, and then criticize that. They look for the problems, and then they say, "We really can't have this! You've got to fix this; this is really not good enough." But that approach causes resentment on the part of the person who's being criticized. What works better is recognition, acknowledgment, and appreciation. So, when I'm driving in to work, I might tell myself: "I'm deliberately going to build a culture of acknowledgment here—where people feel recognized for every little thing they do. They will feel visible, and they will feel as if they're appreciated and acknowledged. I want them to know that what they do is being seen, is being thought about, and is being celebrated. That is the culture that I will create to grow productivity." Whenever possible, recognize those people in front of other people. And if possible, recognize them in front of their families, somehow. You can always send an award or a note from the company president to the person's home. You'll want to let that person's family see that he or she is really appreciated.

63

Seize Responsibility

Ninety-nine percent of failures come from people who have a habit of making excuses. —George Washington Carver "I sure wish people would take responsibility around here!" one of the attorneys in Scott Richardson's law firm said to him. "It seems like the people I'm managing are 'pass the buck' artists." "Well, have you talked to them about what responsibility is?" Scott replied. "Not really," the attorney said.

"Play a little word game with me for a second. I will say a word, and you tell me the first word that pops into your head. Fair enough?" "Oh boy, here we go." "No, this will be useful. I promise." "Okay, shoot. What's the word?" "What's the first word that comes to mind when you hear the word responsibility?" "Obligation," said the attorney. "Great," said Scott. "Now let's break down the word responsibility into its component parts. It literally is response ability or the ability to respond. The ability to do something! Responsible is response-able or being able to respond. That's all responsibility is. Nothing more and nothing less. Responsibility doesn't have anything to do with obligation or the host of other negative words that are associated with it, words that have an intimidating connotation, such as obligation, burden, debt, guilt, fault, and so on. If you want your people to take responsibility, you need to be clear yourself and with them that responsibility doesn't have anything to do with those other words. It is simply the ability to respond, the ability to do something. Just tell your people you believe in them. That you know they have the ability to respond to this challenge, and you support them in doing so." Steve Hardison is a life coach extraordinaire we've worked with and written about extensively in previous books (visit him at: www.theultimatecoach.net). One time Hardison was invited to attend a board meeting of a company he was considering coaching. The first item on the agenda was "Whose fault is it that we have a $100,000 computer system that is a piece of junk?"

The president turned to one of the vice presidents and said, "Joe, this is all your fault!" Joe quickly responded, "No, it's not. I didn't draw up the specs. John did!" John quickly responded, "Hey, wait a minute. I didn't choose the vendor. Rose did." Rose said, "Hey, that wasn't really my decision, I just gave my recommendation to you!" And so the people at the board meeting just kept passing the buck around and around the boardroom. Finally, coach Hardison motioned to the CEO and interrupted the conversation. "Can I say something?" he asked the CEO. "Sure, what?" "I am responsible for the computer system," announced Hardison. "What?" shot back the CEO. "We barely even know who you are! Why would you say anything so crazy?" "Someone needs to be responsible!" said Hardison. "Oh, yeah," replied the CEO. Once Hardison had taken responsibility for the computer system, he was able to lead the discussion on how to move forward and solve the problem. This is true response ability rather than responsibility = blame. Hardison wanted to have the ability to move the problem into a solution mode. Another one of our affiliate coaches started as a salesperson at a high-tech company. In less than two years, he was the CEO. When he was asked how he did it, he said, "I considered it my company from day one. If I saw a piece of paper on the floor, I either picked it up or got someone to do it. If there were a division of the company that was not working, I got involved and got it running better, even though technically it had nothing to do with my job. After a while, they asked me to be the CEO, but I had already taken responsibility for the entire company long before." So if you would like to be the CEO someday, start from this moment taking 100-percent responsibility for the entire company. Nothing will motivate your people more than that.

64

Get some coaching yourself

A teacher affects eternity. He can never tell where his influence stops. —Henry B. Adams, American Historian Great coaches always cite the coaches from whom they themselves have learned. In today's environment, most of today's top business leaders (surveys show more than 70 percent) have coaches—personal success coaches or life coaches—who take them to higher levels of success than they ever could have attained on their own. The object of the coaching process is to allow the leader to discover his or her hidden strengths and to bring them to the forefront in the daily life of the business. Every great actor, dancer, and athlete credits most of their career progress to a coach who gave them support and teaching along the way. In the past, our society celebrated the concept of coaching in sports and show business, because those were fields where excellence was always expected. On the other hand, business was just business. But now because of the growth of coaching, today's business leader has the same opportunity to explore the upper limits of his or her excellence as does a sports star or an actor. Coaching makes that opportunity a conscious part of the leader's career. "I absolutely believe that people, unless coached, never reach their maximum capabilities," said Bob Nardelli, former CEO of Home Depot. If you're a leader, be open to being coached. There's no value in going it alone just to prove you can.

65

Make it happen today

What would be the use of immortality to a person who cannot use well a half an hour? —Ralph Waldo Emerson The ability to motivate others well flows from the importance that we attach to the concept of today. What can we do today? John Wooden was the most successful college basketball coach of all time. His UCLA teams won 10 national championships in a 12-year time span. Wooden created a major portion of his coaching and living philosophy from one thought—a single sentence passed on to him by his father when Wooden was a little boy: "Make each day your masterpiece." While other coaches would try to focus their players on important games in the future, Wooden always focused on today. His practice sessions at UCLA were every bit as important as any championship game. In his philosophy, there was no reason not to make today the proudest day of your life. There was no reason not to play as well in practice as you do in a game. He wanted every player to go to bed each night thinking, "Today, I was at my best." Most of us, however, don't want to live this way. The future is where our happiness lies. So we project things into the future. The past is where the problem began, so we also spend lots of time in the past. But every good thing that has ever happened, happened now, right now. Leadership takes place now, too. Today is your whole life in miniature. You were "born" when you woke up, and you'll "die" when you go to sleep. It was designed this way so that you could live your whole life in a day. Do you still want to walk around telling your team you're having a bad day? When your people see you making each day your masterpiece, they will pick it up as a way to live and work.

66

Learn the inner thing

Your vision will become clear only when you can look into your own heart. Whoever looks outside only dreams, whoever looks inside also awakens. —Carl Jung

Most managers and leaders in this country subconsciously use a Western model of macho warfare for leadership. It is an ineffective model. Scott studied kung fu in Taiwan, and his instructor taught him about inner forces in every human being that can be called on to achieve great things. As Scott rose to prominence as an attorney and a consultant, he credited his martial arts training for much of his insight. Scott recalls: I saw demonstrations when I was in Taiwan and the United States of kung fu masters who, for instance, set up three candles. They had a piece of clear glass in between their face and the candles, so they couldn't blow on the candles. And they proceeded to, in what looked like slow motion, move their fist toward the flame, and from a distance of at least 12 inches, put out these flames. One of my friends, a black belt in karate, watched the demonstration with me. He turned to me and said, "Scott, you've studied kung fu, haven't you?" I said, "A little bit." And he said, "How do they do that? I'm a black belt in karate and one of our tests is we have to be able to put out a candle flame with our strongest kick. We can come as close to the candle flame as we can, and I had to train hours and hours to do that. It's physically impossible to do it from 12 inches away with the strongest kick I have. I could never do it with a slow-motion punch. How do those guys do it?" I replied, "Well, actually it's based on something called 'ki.'" In this conversation, in this moment, now that I think about it, I can now extend ki, and change my body posture slightly and be practicing the advanced martial art of aikido, which I'm just doing as I became aware of it. So with any activity involving a physical body, you can be practicing a version of this martial art aikido. The basic principles of extending ki include focusing on your one point and thinking about that. In aikido, they teach you that if you focus your attention on your one point, which is a point 2 inches below your navel, you automatically are centered. That's all you have to do. You can do it in a team meeting. You can do it during a one-on-one performance review. There's no great mystery about it. The aikido instructor does a demonstration where he says, "Okay, focus on your one point," and while you're focused on your ki point below the navel, he presses on your chest but you don't fall over. You're very centered and strong. Then if he lightly slaps you on the top of your head with one hand (to change your focus) then pushes on your chest with the other, you do immediately fall over backwards. And he says, "What just happened? You had your awareness on your one point and, when you did, I couldn't push you over. And then as soon as I slapped you on the top of your head, what happened? Your awareness went up there to your head and I pushed you over without even trying." I did this simple demonstration to my father, the doctor—the world's biggest skeptic—and he said, "There must be a physical explanation for it." But there was not. He hadn't moved a muscle in his body! Nothing physical. Just his focus. And that was the difference between his being grounded and centered and strong, and then losing focus.

Most people in the workplace are not centered. They live off the top of their heads where, basically, anything that comes up in life is going to tip them over. Tip them off center. As their leader, you can model being centered. You can radiate the immovable life force, the ki inside you. In your next managerial challenge, try relaxing and allowing a force greater than yourself to flow through you and then out into the situation. And it won't be long before you, too, are a legend in your organization, for simply being centered.

67

Forget about failure

A life spent making mistakes is not only more honorable but more useful than a life spent in doing nothing. —George Bernard Shaw Managers, especially at the beginning of their careers, often obsess about failure. They take a bad conversation with a problem employee very personally. They get hurt. They get depressed. They get angry and start hating their profession. But soon they see that failure is just an outcome. It is not bad or good, just neutral. It can be turned into something good if it's studied for the wisdom to be gained from it. And it can be turned into something bad if it is made into something personal. The great professor of linguistics S.I. Hayakawa used to say that there were basically two kinds of people: the kind of person who fails at something and says, "I failed at that" and the person who fails at something and says, "I'm a failure." The first person is in touch with the truth, and the second person is not. "I'm a failure!" That claim doesn't always appear to the outsider to be a lie. It can look like a sad form of self-acceptance. In fact, we can even associate such exaggerating with truthful confession: "Why not admit it? I'm a failure." But in psychological terms, what we're hearing is the voice of fear. It's the opposite of a voice of purpose; it is a voice of surrender, of internal defeat, of quitting before I begin. (Defeat and failure on the external can actually be refreshing and rejuvenating. The great football coach Woody Hayes used to say after his team lost a game, "Nothing cleanses the soul like getting the hell kicked out of you.") As you lead people today, always keep in mind this one true fact: there is nothing wrong with them. They have it inside themselves to prosper and excel as professionals. Get connected to that truth and show your people how to leave all their "I'm a failure" thoughts in the trash where they belong.

68

Follow consulting with action

Action is eloquence. —Shakespeare Scott has been practicing law for more than 20 years, had his own law firm for 17 years, and even owned another

law firm, which he sold during that time. Right now, he has 15 employees and he coaches other lawyers as well. He states: There's no question in my mind that it is one thing to be a coach, another thing to be in the role of the CEO. I think the perspective of being the one in the hot seat, so to speak, is extremely valuable. Having been both roles, I have coached and been coached, I know a coach can be absolutely invaluable to the person in the hot seat. But you can bring in the world's greatest coach, and if the person in the hot seat still chooses, for whatever reason, not to take the coaching, then the effort is lost. That's the reason leaders are the most important people in the organization, because they can choose not to make things happen as well as to make things happen. A coach is not going to wave a magic wand and cause things to change regardless of that decision. It can't work that way. In the end, a coach can only shine a light and assist. It's always the willingness of the leader to generate the action that makes a true difference. So if you are getting coaching, follow it up with action. Massive action. To do so will be eloquent.

69

Create a vision

The reason most major goals are not achieved is that we spend our time doing second things first. —Robert J. McKain, Management Consultant Without creating a vision for my team, my team will live according to its problems. Without goals (the subsets of vision), my team will just fight fires, work through emotional upsets, and worry about the dysfunctional behavior of other people. I, myself, as their leader, will have attracted a problem-based existence. Soon, I will only end up doing what I feel like doing, which will sell me short and draw on the smallest of my own brain's resources. But when we humans begin to create, we use more of the brain. We rise up to our highest functioning as humans. So it's my primary job as a motivator to create a vision of who we want to be, and then live in that picture as if it were already happening in this very moment. And it has to be a vision I can talk about every day. It can't be a framed statement on the wall that no one can relate to after some company retreat is over. It is not surprising that one of the biggest complaints about leaders that show up on employee surveys is, "He had no idea where we were headed. He had no vision of our future that he could tell us about." Create a vision. Live the vision.

70

Stop looking over shoulder

Courage is not the absence of fear, but rather the judgment that something else is more important than fear. —Ambrose Redmoon, American Philosopher There's no one less motivational to be around than someone who is always trying to anticipate other people's criticisms.

The worst trap for you as a leader is to begin anticipating what your own leaders think of you from moment to moment, to do superficial things to impress them, rather than doing real things to encourage your own people. Great leadership by example (such a great motivator of others) comes from getting independently better at what you do, and not living in anticipation of other people's opinion of you. It allows you to increase your leadership strength every day, and to build your self-esteem. Paradoxically, the more you focus on doing your own best work and staying in action to fulfill your personal and professional goals, the more help you are to others.

71

Lead yourself by selling

Everyone lives by selling something. —Robert Louis Stevenson Dan Kennedy is a local marketing expert who has done a lot of direct sales in his lifetime. He has made the observation that the most successful doctors, lawyers, teachers, and businesspeople that he works with invariably have some sales experience in their background. Scott recalls: I was wondering, before, why I've never had a problem enrolling people in projects. It's just been very easy for me, always. And then I heard Dan Kennedy's observation: You know, he's right! Before I had had some direct sales experience, I was very poor at enrolling people in projects and ideas. Afterward, I was great. So let me tell you how I experienced that transformation in my life.

Before I went to college, I decided to spend a summer selling books door-to-door in Pennsylvania. I attended a week-long sales training school put on by a company called Southwestern, the largest door-to-door book sales company in the United States. (They primarily use college students to work during the summer.) During this week, we learned our basics. It was the old-style selling: You learned your sales pitch and memorized it. Then you learned about door approaches, how to inspire confidences and get in and make your presentation, and how to close (gracefully asking for the order). Just classic selling. The very first house I called on, I actually sold something. And I thought, Man, this stuff really works. This is a piece of cake. And that was the last sale I had for two weeks. And so my sales manager decided to start working with me to see what wasn't working. He gave me a diagnosis, "Scott, you're not closing. You're not even asking for the sale." "What do you mean I'm not closing? Of course I'm closing." "No, you're not. You didn't close once." "I didn't?" "No. Look, I know we taught you to close at least three times, but for you there's no limit. Just start off showing them a little bit about the books, then you close. And if they say, 'No, I'm not interested,' you say, 'I know just what you mean,' and you show them a little bit more, and you close again." So I said, "That's crazy. They're going to throw me out on my butt!"

"Just try it." Well, I figured the other way wasn't working, so what the heck? So the next house we called on, I presented the books a little bit and asked the lady for the order. She said, "Well, I'm really not interested." "That's fine, I know exactly what you mean," I said. Then I showed her a little bit more and asked her again. And she said, "Well, I don't know, I don't have the money." "I know exactly what you mean," I said. And I showed her a little bit more and closed her again. I closed her at least five times and I thought, Man, how long is this going to take? I guess she hasn't kicked me out, so I'll keep going. And finally, I think on the sixth close, she said, "Okay!" I was shocked. Later on, something very surprising happened. It turned out that this nice lady worked in a bank right there in Gettysburg, Pennsylvania. One day, when I went to the bank to bring all my checks from my sales to deposit, I saw her there. She was working as a teller. I put my checks in to deposit, and she seemed very embarrassed to see me. So I thought, Oh my gosh, maybe I just ramrodded her into buying and now she feels bad. But oh well, we always tell them they can cancel the order. So I shoved my checks toward her and said, "I want to deposit these checks." And she said, "You know, Scott, I hope you didn't mind that I took so long to decide, but I just wanted to make sure that I really wanted those books. Now I'm so glad I bought them."

What a lesson. So from then on, I've never been afraid to ask. And then ask again! In terms of leadership, this simply means asking for what you want, being very direct with your requests, and having your communication centered on requests and promises. You can go up the ladder to the people who lead you and make bold requests on behalf of you and your team. You can do the same with major customers. Also, with your own direct reports, figure out what you want your people to buy in to, and then sell them on the idea. But don't forget to close them. Don't forget to make a strong, specific request (the close), and then receive a strong, specific promise in return.

72

Hold on the principle

In matters of style, swim with the current; in matters of principle, stand like a rock. —Thomas Jefferson "Discipline yourself, and others won't need to," Coach John Wooden would tell his players. "Never lie. Never cheat. Never steal," and "Earn the right to be proud and confident." We're starting to learn why John Wooden was the most successful college basketball coach of all time. No one has ever even come close. No one has ever motivated his athletes so superbly as Wooden. Rick Reilly, the talented sportswriter, recalls ("A Paradigm Rising above the Madness," Sports Illustrated, March 20, 2000): "If you played for him, you played by his rules:Never score without acknowledging a teammate. One word of profanity, and you're done for the day. Treat your opponent with respect. Coach Wooden believed in hopelessly out-of-date stuff that never did anything but win championships." Reilly writes that Coach Wooden's rule that his players could not have long hair or facial hair particularly drove them crazy. When Bill Walton, an All-American center, showed up with a full beard, he said, "It's my right." Reilly goes on: "Coach Wooden asked if he believed that strongly. Walton said he did. 'That's good, Bill,' Coach said. 'I admire people who have strong beliefs and stick by them, I really do. We're going to miss you.' Walton shaved it right then and there. Now Walton calls once a week to tell Coach he loves him." You have two ways to go as a motivator of others. You can seek to be liked or you can, like John Wooden, earn their respect. Respect is stronger. And, when their respect runs deep enough, you may end up being loved.

73

Create Your Relationships

A life of reaction is a life of slavery, intellectually and spiritually. One must fight for a life of action, not reaction. —Rita Mae Brown, Mystery Author When we are coaching leaders who are having a tough time motivating others, it always becomes apparent that their basic problem is that they're reacting to their people all day long.They're wallowing in their own negative emotional reaction to people. After a while, in listening to these types of managers, we get a funny impression that we're listening to the words of country music. You know those country songs we're talking about. The themes are: "I've been hurt so many times, I'm never going to reach out again," or "I don't trust women," or "You can't trust men." Actual songs have titles such as "Is It Cold in Here or Is It You?" and "My Wife Ran Away With My Best Friend and I Miss Him." Country music in and of itself is great, and the really sad songs—the ones that express the poetry of victimization— are beautiful in their own way, but their basic philosophy is not an effective way to create the motivated team we want. Managers who go through their days reacting emotionally to the behavior of their people truly are miserable. What those managers need is a gentle shift. Not a huge change, but a shift, just like the gentle shift of gears in a finely tuned car. They need to shift from reacting to creating. All of this reacting they do has become a habit, and because it's only a habit, it's completely open to a shift. Business coach Dan Sullivan nails it when he says, "The difficulty in changing habits lies in the fact that we are changing something that feels completely natural to us. Good habits feel natural; bad habits feel natural. That is the nature of a habit. When you change a bad habit that feels natural to a good habit that feels natural, you feel exactly the same. It is just that you get completely different results." One of the first steps on the path out of the habit of reacting to the people we manage is to ask ourselves a simple question. It's a question first asked by Ralph Waldo Emerson many years ago: "Why should my happiness depend on the thoughts going on in someone else's head?" This question, no matter how we answer it in any given moment, gives us the mental perspective we need to start seeing the possibilities for creatively relating to others instead of just reacting to them.

74

Don't Make Request

As you enter positions of trust and power, dream a little before you think. —Toni Morrison, Author Don't you wish you could just ask your superiors to help your team do certain things? It would make leadership much simpler if it could become a matter of requests and promises and follow-through action. It can. It will help you to know, before you ask, that everyone (your superiors, your customers, your employees) really wants to say yes. We once took a seminar on communication, and one of the exercises they gave us was designed to dramatize the fact that most people really want to say yes. So they gave us an assignment over a long dinner break to go out and make three unreasonable requests to see if we could get people to say no. That was the assignment: you had to get three "no" responses before you came back. And we thought it would be simple. After Scott finished dinner, he went over to a lady at the next table and said, "You know, ma'am, I'm completely out of money, would you mind paying for my meal?" He figured that was a pretty unreasonable request and he was sure she'd say, "Get lost." And he was stunned when she didn't say that. "Well, I'm not sure I have enough money to cover that right now," she said, so Scott began coaching her to say no. "Oh that's okay, just asking. You can say no." And she wouldn't say no! She said, "Well, I'm not sure...." "In other words, 'no'?" "Well, I guess not. No." "Thanks!" Scott had to work very hard just to get her to say no. Then when Scott walked over to the cashier to pay for the meal, there was a man who was waiting there and Scott thought, No problem. I'll get a quick "No" from him. "You know, I'm a little short on cash," Scott said. "Would you just have the restaurant cover my bill?" "Well, I'm not sure. What's this about?" "Well, you can say no." It took him quite awhile (soon Scott was begging him for a no), but he finally got him to say no. Two down, one to go. So Scott turned to the lady right next to him and said, "How about you? Would you pick up my bill?" She had just heard what went on, so it didn't look like it would be too hard! But it was. And after a very long negotiation, after she was quite willing to pay for his meal, she said no. That one exercise taught us a lot. People all want to say yes. So now, whenever we have a project that we want to create, we feel free inside to go out there and start asking people for a "yes." We don't have any fear or hesitancy in making what most people would call "unreasonable requests." Because we know from experience (after having it verified many times over) that people's natural tendency is to want to say yes. So ask for what you want, both up and down the pecking order. If your team needs something from the higherups, go ask for it. When you get their yes answers, bring in good news for your team about what the top people are agreeing to do to move things forward. You'll be teaching them the power of requests.

75

Don't change yourself

It takes a tremendous act of courage to admit to yourself that you are not defective in any way whatsoever. —Cheri Huber, Author/Zen Philosopher

You don't need to change! A lot of people who hear our talks or read our books contact us for coaching, saying, "I really need to make a change. I need to totally change my life. I have been an unconscious, bossy, paranoid manager and I'm ready to learn to be a leader."

We tell them what we tell everyone: You don't need to totally "change." All you need is a gentle shift. To get your sports car to send itself into a smoother, faster gear, do you need to take out the gearbox and put in a new one? Or do you simply need to shift gears? When you do shift gears, is it hard to do? Hard, like changing a tire? Or do you just slide into it? For your mind to take you to the next level of leadership performance, all you need to do is shift gears. You don't need to replace your gearbox. Just shift. And then zoom. Zoom. Just like that. Do you need to change your attitude? How? Why? What is an attitude anyway? How do you change it? Attitude is a word that old people use to intimidate young people. It's the ultimate shaming device: "You better change your attitude, Son!" "How, Dad?" "Don't mess with me, Son." "What is attitude, Dad? How do I access it? How do I even identify it, much less change it?" "It's poor, I can tell you that." If you were ever part of such a conversation, you got off on the wrong track in this whole concept of change. Reinventing yourself happens. But it happens as a result of a series of gentle shifts. It's a path, not a revolution. It becomes a way of life. Just begin.

76

Pump up Your Email

No pessimist ever discovered the secrets of the stars, or sailed to an uncharted land, or opened a new heaven to the human spirit. —Helen Keller Every e-mail communication you send to your team is an opportunity. It's a fresh chance to energize that team and spread the optimism you want to fuel the contagious enthusiasm your next project needs. But nine managers out of 10 ignore this opportunity. Instead, they often send neutral e-mails; short, terse e-mails; or sometimes even angry e-mails. Those are all mistakes. Because your first job, even before your job of informing others, is to motivate others. So let's begin here: realize that e-mail is a cold medium anyway. There is no voice tone in it. There is no twinkle in the eye, or warmth of expression. It's just cold electronic type. Therefore, even a neutral e-mail feels chilly to the recipient. Even a simple transfer of information feels icy and negative, unless you seize the opportunity to pump it up. Always pump it up. Every communication from a manager to an employee is an opportunity to instill optimism. Don't waste that opportunity. A true leader never does. Look at your e-mail before you send it. Is it uplifting? Does it contain an acknowledgment or an appreciation of the recipient? Does it praise the recipient? Does it inspire? Is it going to make someone happy?

If not, take the extra minute to go back over it. Change the negative tone to a positive one. Brighten it up. Ask yourself: Would you be happy to get this e-mail? Would you feel honored and appreciated if you received it? Behavioral studies continue to show that positive reinforcement works more than seven times better than negative criticism to change behavior. Negative criticism causes resentment, depression, anger, and sabotage. People will sabotage your leadership if they feel alienated and underappreciated. Pump things up and watch what happens. Don't take this on faith; use trial and error. Send half of your people a neutral e-mail and half a positive one, and see which gets the best results. You will be able to test this concept by doing it. You will be delighted with the results you get.

77

Stop pushing

Pull the string, and it will follow wherever you wish. Push it, and it will go nowhere at all. —Dwight D. Eisenhower Thomas Crum gives seminars on how to use aikido philosophy in daily business life. He calls what he teaches "The magic of conflict." Scott remembers being there during one of Crum's demonstrations. Crum had someone come to the front of the room and stand up in front of him.

"Put out your hand like this," said Crum as he put his hand up as if taking an oath, touching the student's upraised hand. Crum pushed on the student's upraised hand, and the student just naturally, automatically reacted by pushing back. Crum said, "That's the natural way of human beings. I push, you give me resistance. You push back." Then, he asked the student to extend his hand in the form of a fist. He did, and then Crum put his hand in a closed fist in front of him and they both pushed against each other. Each fist pushing the other. "This is the way we experience life a lot," said Crum. "Just like this. A stalemate or struggle, where I'm trying to win or you're trying to win. In aikido, we don't ever resist." Right at that moment Crum dropped his fist down, and instantly the volunteer pushed right by him (and, in aikido, you turn in the direction of the person going by you). Crum turned with the volunteer and guided him quickly and gently to the floor. Crum said, "Now, this is aikido. I no longer resist, so we're no longer fighting. And guess what? We're in perfect alignment so it's very easy for me to direct this person wherever I choose him to go. And that's how aikido works." In fact, the characters ai, ki, and do mean blending our inner forces, not force against force. And every move in aikido comes to that point, where both the aggressor's ki and your own ki are blended. Right at that point, when the two are in alignment, I have control over the other person and what happens to him and his body. Totally. It takes no effort. Because we're in complete alignment. The application to motivating others is profound, because I don't really want to resist what my people are doing or saying. I want to guide their natural inner energy toward a mutual goal, theirs and mine. I want to receive and guide my people's natural energy. I don't want to oppose it or make it wrong.

A boss creates fear, a leader, confidence. A boss fixes blame, a leader corrects mistakes. A boss knows all, a leader asks questions. A boss makes work drudgery, a leader makes it interesting. —Russell H. Ewing, Author If I'm an unconscious manager, can I be taught to be a true leader? Of course I can. If you are going to turn me into a true leader, you begin by making what is unconscious (my commitments and operating principles as a leader) become conscious and clear. That's step one. That process is as simple as teaching me how to use a computer program. Perhaps you hold a leadership meeting and state very clearly why and how you intend to lead. You make everything clear. If there are other leaders in the room, even leaders whom you lead, you invite them to do the same. The more open we all are about how we intend to lead, the more motivated our people will be. One of the exercises we like to do in our leadership seminars is to ask people to write down the name of someone in their lives whom they admired and respected as a leader. It may be their grandmother, an old platoon leader, or a former teacher or manager. Some people write down a leader in history who had an influence on them, such as John F. Kennedy or Winston Churchill. You might want to do this exercise right now. Think of someone in your own life you respected as a leader. Jot the name down. Now, write three qualities about that person that you admired the most. Don't read on until you do. Okay, now look at those three qualities. They may be anything—honesty, openness, a total belief in you, creativity, nonjudgmental teaching style—whatever the three qualities are, look at them. More than likely, and more than nine times out of 10, these qualities are now in you as a leader. And these are the three things your people would say about you! Look at them. Is it not true? Are they not who you are? This is a powerful exercise because it shows you how you have already internalized and modeled yourself after the leaders you admired. But until now, it has been subconscious. The trick is to make it conscious, and be very awake to it every day. There is nothing so disheartening as a leader having a perceived hidden agenda, which comes from overly unconscious values at play. It discourages your people when they have to guess where you're coming from every day. Far better to have both you and your people fully conscious of what you stand for.

78

Come From Future

The very essence of leadership is that you have to have vision. You can't blow an uncertain trumpet. —Theodore M. Hesburgh, Former President, Notre Dame

Managers often, quite unconsciously, allow team meetings and one-on-one conferences to focus excessively on the past. But the constant refrain of how things used to be and why things were "better back then" demoralizes the team. The team also sits through unnecessarily long periods of time spent hashing out, venting, and reviewing breakdowns and mistakes. This is done at the expense of the future. It is also done at the expense of optimism, morale, and a sense of good, orderly direction. A good motivator will not make the mistake of obsessive focus on the past. A good motivator will use the past as a springboard that immediately leads to a discussion of the future: "What can we learn from that mistake that will serve us in the future? And if this happens again, how might we handle it better?" To a good motivator, the past really has only one purpose: to provide building material for creating the future. The past is not used as something to get hung up on, or an excuse for regret, placing blame, nostalgia, personal attacks, and having a defeated attitude. A leader knows that leadership means leading people into the future. Just as a scout leader leads scouts into the woods, a true leader leads team members into the future. Your shift to better leadership might include learning to make an ever-increasing percentage of your communication focus on the future: discussing your next week, planning your next month, designing your goals for next year, and looking at the opportunities that will be there two years from now. Be thorough and well-prepared when it comes to discussing the future. If the details are not always known, the commitments, vision, and strategies are.Unmotivational managers will unconsciously disown and spread fear about the future. They will say how unpredictable and dangerous the future is. They will exaggerate potential problems and stress the unpredictability of everything. They will attempt to come across as realists when, in fact, it's much more truthful to say that they simply haven't done their homework. You'll be motivating others to the degree that you are a constant source of information and interesting communication about the future of the team.

79

Teach them to teach themselves

If you want a man to be for you, never let him feel he is dependent on you. Make him feel you are in some way dependent on him. —General George C. Marshall Scott remembers a story that Mr. Mercado told him about the musical virtuoso Jascha Heifetz and the always unplayable Tchaikovsky violin concerto. Heifetz's teacher was the great German violinist Leopold Auer. Mercado said, "Auer himself could not play the Tchaikovsky violin concerto up to speed. It'd never been performed up to speed before Heifetz." Heifetz was the first one to perform this piece up to speed! And if Auer, his teacher, could not perform it up to speed, and he was teaching Heifetz, how then was Heifetz able to do it? Some people might say, "Well, he was just a talent."

But that wasn't the explanation according to Mr. Mercado. He said, "Scott, if Auer was only teaching Heifetz how to play like Auer, then Heifetz would have never performed that Tchaikovsky violin concerto up to speed. But that isn't what Auer was doing. He was teaching him how to teach himself how to play the instrument. And that's how he learned to become better than his teacher." This is a very powerful distinction. And that really is why Auer was such an extraordinary teacher. Your goal is to teach like Leopold Auer taught, absolutely unafraid of the people you lead being better than you are. Because that's what a great coach and leader does. They don't teach us how to have a great career. They teach us how to teach ourselves how to have a great career.

If the rate of change on the outside exceeds the rate of change on the inside, the end is near. —Jack Welch Managers who apologize for any and all changes the team must accommodate are sowing the seeds of low morale and discouragement. Every time they introduce a new policy, product, system, rule, or project, they apologize for it. They imply that change is harmful to the well-being of the team and that change is something we would hope someday to not have to suffer so much of. This is done with the unconscious motive of seeming compassionate, and being liked, but it results in creating a team of victims, and it dramatically lengthens the time it takes for the team to assimilate and become comfortable with a change. A true leader does not apologize for change. A true leader does not feed into the fear that so easily accompanies change. Instead, the leader is an advocate for the change. A leader continuously communicates the benefits of having an ever-changing organization. A leader endorses an organization that is continuously reinventing itself to higher and higher levels of productivity and innovation. Every change is made for a reason. Every change was decided upon because the positives of the change outweigh the negatives. So, if you wish to be a highly motivational leader, you simply learn the positives, through and through. You find out everything there is to know about the upside of the change, because that's what leadership is. Leadership is communication of the upside. Unconscious managers are often as uncomfortable with changes as their own people are, so they constantly apologize for them, which furthers the impression that this little team is not in alignment with the mission of the company. But not you. You are a leader, and so you will always reconnect the team to the mission of the company. Change will not be apologized for. Why apologize for something that will improve the strength of the organization? Every change is made (every last one of them) for the sole purpose of strengthening the ultimate viability of the organization. That's why you advocate the change. That's how you sell it to your team.

80

Let People Find it.

People ask the difference between a leader and a boss. The leader works in the open, and the boss in covert. The leader leads and the boss drives. —Theodore Roosevelt Scott again recalls coach and teacher Rodney Mercado and his master key to getting remarkable performances out of the people he taught and motivated: If you heard any two students of Mercado play side by side, you would absolutely swear that they did not have the same teacher. You would say it was physically impossible because their playing styles were so radically different. Most people who take music lessons are aware that listeners can identify who a student's teacher is by how the student plays. But with Mercado, not only could you not do that, you would absolutely swear that they couldn't have the same teacher, that it just couldn't be possible. So how did he accomplish that? For one thing, he never told us "don't," he never said no, and he never told us how to play the instrument. A typical example, a very fundamental thing, was how to hold the bow. He would say, "Okay, Scott, what I'd like you to do is to try holding your hand this way," and he'd have me adopt an extreme position, like holding my hand as far to the right as I possibly could while still being able to use my bow. He'd have me play some music that way, and then say, "Okay, fine. Now I'd like you to do the opposite," and he'd have me put my hand all the way to the left, as far as I could possibly put it—a very uncomfortable position—and then he'd say, "Play this passage." He would then ask, "Now, if you had to choose one of those two extremes, which one would you choose?" "Well, all the way to the right, because it's a little less cumbersome than all the way to the left." "So what that's telling you, Scott, is that you probably want to hold your hand position somewhere between all the way to the right and all the way to the left, and it's probably going to be more to the right than to the left. So find the way that works the best for you." And if I said, "Well, what about if other people say you have to hold your hand a certain way?" Mercado would then reel off a number of examples of professional violinists who did it differently. He'd ask me to reason it out. "So what is that telling you, Scott?" "Well, that there isn't one right way to do it." "Right, so find what works for you." And that was his teaching method. So, I learned from that, and in motivating people I adapted it to mean that there is never one right way to do something. Rather than showing my people the "right way" to make a phone call, or gather information from a client, I will let them develop their own ways. The lesson learned for me way back in music class was that people will motivate themselves in their own way if you gently guide them toward the outcome you want.

81

Be A Optimist

A leader is a dealer in hope. —Napoleon Bonaparte Pessimism is the most fundamental of all the mistakes we managers can make. It is a position, a pose, taken by the manager of not being optimistic about the future of the organization and, therefore, the future of the team. It is a refusal to prepare for team meetings by learning the rationale behind the latest company decisions. It is a refusal to take a stand for the success of the enterprise. It is a refusal to be an advocate for the organization's ongoing strategy. It is also an exaggerated tendency to acknowledge and agree with every issue's downside without standing up for the upside. Sometimes optimism is a lonely and courageous position to take, which is why most managers don't do it. The sad thing is, it is what the team wants and needs the most from its leader. While the unconscious manager doesn't realize what he or she is doing by being so pessimistic all the time, a true leader knows exactly what optimism is and what it is for: Optimism is the practice of focusing on opportunities and possibilities rather than complaints and fears. A true optimist is not a brainless Pollyanna, wearing rose-colored glasses. A true optimist is more realistic than that. A true optimist is unafraid of confronting and understanding the problems in the organization. But once a problem is fully identified and understood, the optimist returns the thinking to opportunity and possibility.

Optimistic leaders acknowledge the downside of every situation, then focus the majority of their thinking on the upside. They also focus the majority of their communication on the upside. They know that the downside is always well-known throughout the team. But the upside is never as well-known. Who wants to look like an idiotic optimist? It is far more popular and easy to be a clever and witty pessimist. But it is not leadership.

Optimism in the face of a grumbling and pessimistic team takes courage and energy. It is something most team members would never be willing to do. It is the heart and soul of leadership. And while you may be questioned about it now and then, in the end, the very end, when your work is almost through, it is what your team members will love you for the most.

Do not hope wholly to reason away your troubles; do not feed them with attention, and they will die imperceptibly away. Fix your thoughts upon your business, fill your intervals with company, and sunshine will again break in upon your mind. —Samuel Johnson Anything you pay attention to expands. It grows. Pay attention to your house plants and they grow. Pay attention to your favorite cause, and your passion and knowledge will grow the success of that cause. Attention is like that. Anywhere you direct it, the object of that attention grows. When you talk to members of your team, keep paying attention to the end results you want, not the effort to achieve them. When you praise your managers, pay attention to results they achieved that you wanted, not the trying, the effort, or the attempt to do it. Most managers miss this vital point; they keep rewarding the "trying," not realizing that doing so sends the subconscious message that "trying" is always enough. Their people soon think that if they can show they're making efforts, if they can show activity, then there won't be so much focus on end results. Make sure you reward end results more than anything else. If you do so, you'll get better end results. You have to be the one who keeps talking numbers if you want that one person to hit his numbers. If, instead, you commiserate with how hard everything is, and you acknowledge how hard everyone is trying, then that's what you'll get: fewer results and more trying. Whatever you praise, grows. Always. It's the law of the harvest. Attention is powerful. Yet most people allow their attention to be pushed and pulled around all day long by outside forces. A chance phone call. Some annoying e-mail. Somebody walking by their desk and asking a loaded question. Attention gets spread too thinly this way. But your attention is like money. It is a precious treasure. It is paid in to things. We say pay attention for a reason. It is invested. It gets paid in to whatever you choose to pay it in to. If you pay it in to the things you want (measurable, numerical outcomes and specific results), you will get more and more of what you want.

82

Create a routine

Patience and perseverance have a magical effect before which difficulties disappear and obstacles vanish. —John Quincy Adams Leadership success is not easy, but it is not all that hard, either. It is not nearly as hard as we often make it for ourselves. The major psychological obstacle to motivational success is the myth of permanent characteristics. It is people who think that their habits of action are not habits, but permanent traits. Believing in that totally false myth traps managers in a prison, an iron web of limitation. And it's all unnecessary! The repeated action patterns that you and I demonstrate throughout the day are a result of habit, not the result of permanent characteristics, or character defects, or hard-wired personality traits. If we don't like a certain tendency someone has (let's say to procrastinate having that important talk with a coworker), then the first step in correcting the tendency is to see it for what it is: a habit. A habit is a pattern of behavior woven into seeming permanence by repetition. If I repeatedly and consistently put off doing the tough tasks in favor of the easy ones, it will become a habit. It's the law of the human neurological system. So, what do we do? All we have to do to build a new habit is to create a routine. That's right, a routine! Please repeat to yourself, "I don't need self-discipline for this, I don't need a new personality, I don't need fresh strength of character or even more willpower. All I Need Is a Routine." Lyndon Duke, one of our top mentors and business productivity coaches, once said that he had spent many years lowering his self-esteem by bemoaning the condition of his chaotic apartment. He lived alone and was a highly active business genius who worked many long and joyful hours, but couldn't keep his place clean. He told himself that he was an undisciplined and disorganized person. Soon, in his own mind, he was a slob. That is a permanent characteristic: slob. Finally it dawned on him that the only thing missing was a routine. That's all he lacked! He didn't lack willpower, good character, or self-control. Not at all! He simply lacked a routine. So he made up a routine: "I will straighten things up for 20 minutes every morning." Mondays, while coffee was brewing, for just a few short and quick minutes, he would do his living room. Tuesdays, his kitchen. Wednesdays, the bedroom. Thursdays, the hall and porch. Fridays, the home office and den. And each Saturday morning, for 20 minutes, he would do a deeper cleaning of his choice. That became his routine. The beauty of a routine is that it eventually becomes habit. "At first, it was awkward and weird," he said. "And I thought to myself that it was so unnatural and uncomfortable that I would probably never follow through, but I promised myself a 90-day free trial. I'd be free to drop it if my theory was incorrect. My theory was that I only needed a routine, and that once my routine became routine, it would be an effortless and natural part of my life." He was absolutely correct about all of it. When we first visited him at his apartment, long after his routine had become habit, we noticed how clean and orderly it looked. We assumed he had someone come in to clean. Then he told us about the power, the absolutely stunning and amazing power, of making up a routine. "I do it so naturally now that sometimes I don't even remember having done it," he said. "So I'll have to look out at my living room to check, and lo and behold, it's in complete order. I had done it without thinking." If something isn't happening in your professional life, if you could be more productive if only you were "as disciplined as so and so," then worry no longer. It isn't about you. It's about your lack of a routine. Make up your routine, and follow your routine, and if you do this for 90 days, it will be so effortless and natural to you that you'll never have to think about it again. Do you hate yourself because you don't prepare for your team meetings? There's nothing wrong with you. You just need a routine. Are you troubled by how your e-mail is taking up your precious time and life as a leader? You aren't missing any kind of inner strength; you are missing a routine. Check your e-mail two specific times a day and tell your people that's what you do. Create a routine for yourself. Follow your routine for 90 days. Then you're free.

Love is always creative and fear is always destructive. If you could only love enough, you would be the most powerful person in the world. —Emmet Fox, Author/Philosopher

The most important principle of motivation is this: You get what you reward. It's true of every relationship. It's true of pets, house plants, children, and lovers. You get what you reward. It's especially true of team motivation. Positive reinforcement of the desired behavior works much faster and much more permanently than criticizing poor behavior. Love conquers fear every time. Leaders who figure out, on their own, ways to reward their people for good performance get more good performances than leaders who run around all day putting out fires caused by their people's poor performance. The reason most people don't maximize this reward concept is that they wait too long to put it into effect. They wait to decide whether to reward people, and soon, before they know it, a big problem comes up to be dealt with. By then it's too late. Dedicate a certain portion of each day to rewarding people, even if it's only a verbal reward. Ten minutes at the end of the day. Get on the phone. Send out some e-mails. Reward. Reward. (Sometimes verbal and written rewards, rather than financial bonuses and prizes, are the ones that go the farthest in inspiring a person to do more.) Obtain a copy of Bob Nelson's excellent study of how companies reward their people, 1001 Ways to Reward Employees, 2nd Edition (Workman Publishing Company, 2005), and read it with a yellow highlighter or a red pen in hand. Everyone we know who does this increases their team's productivity. Everyone we know who does this underlines and highlights completely different parts of the book and then translates the ideas into ideas that fit their style. Most of the ideas don't take any extra time, just extra commitment to reward. But you'll get what you reward.

Nothing so conclusively proves a man's ability to lead others as what he does from day to day to lead himself. —Thomas J. Watson, Former CEO, IBM You'll lead better if you slow down. You'll get more done, too. It doesn't seem like it would be true. It doesn't seem like slowing down would get that much more done. But it does. Every day you do it, you will get more done. Every day you experiment with slowing down, you will understand the truth behind the legend of the tortoise and the hare. The most important element of slowing down is to know that you're always working on the right thing to be working on at any given time. Business consultant Chet Holmes says that he and his clients accomplish that by making sure each day has only six things on the Must Do list. That list lets them slow down. "Why only six things?" says Holmes. "Because with a bigger list than that, generally you just try to trim the list. You spend the day trimming the list. At the end of the day you feel that most of the important things on the list did not get completed. You just look down and say, 'Oh, I didn't do the most important things.' There's a bad psychological impact in not finishing your list! And so only list the six most important things...and then make sure you get them done. You'll be amazed at how much you've accomplished." If I am on the wrong road, it doesn't matter how good I get at speeding down the road. It's still the wrong road. I need to remind myself to slow down and win. I need to take my sweet, gentle time. I want this conversation ahead of me to be relaxed and strong so that the relationship I have becomes relaxed and strong. So all day, it helps to tell myself: Slow down. Even slower than that. There you go.

83

Decide To Be Great

When life demands more of people than they demand of life—as is ordinarily the case—what results is a resentment of life almost as deep-seated as the fear of death. —Tom Robbins, Author Either now or on one's deathbed, one realizes a strange truth: There's no excuse for not being great. If you are a leader, a leader is what you are. If you are still just a manager, just managing to manage, well, maybe you'll manage, but how fulfilling is that? How proud is your subconscious mind of you? How proud is your family? Someday you will just decide to be great at what you do. You'll never look back. You'll never regret the decision. It might not have seemed like a big deal at the moment youdecided, but somehow you'll know the decision is final. It will never have to be revisited. There's a reason why it's good to be great: people want to follow you. People start to respect you. People want to be more like you. People want to do things for you. And if you are honest with yourself, you will someday realize the truth for yourself, either now, or on your deathbed: There was no excuse for not being great.

Everyone thinks of changing the world, but no one thinks of changing himself. —Leo Tolstoy There's a reason why advertisers always look for ways to use real people in "before and after" pictures. Nothing motivates a buyer more! You as a leader can keep tapping into that ultimate motivational tool—your own growth. Your people will always remember what you used to be like, and see what you're like now. Nothing inspires and motivates people as much as watching someone else change for the better. When you are willing to offer yourself up as a role model for personal change, you'll motivate your people faster than anything else you can do. Watch what happens when your team sees you evolve, change, and grow. It's inspiring for them to see that you yourself are not cast in stone, locked in to your own hardened habits of leadership.

It's exciting for people to witness your courageous evolution. When your employee fills out a form that evaluates you as a leader, you want their most telling comment about you to be how they admire your own "willingness to grow." And this growth can take place in absolutely any category. So you never have to stop looking for areas that have potential for you to demonstrate your own willingness to challenge yourself. For example, let's look at your physical condition. Why not? Everyone else is. Does that make you uncomfortable? That they would even notice something like that? They shouldn't! How judgmental! How irrelevant! Well, let's just face up to it. Your physical condition will always be observed by everyone who works for you. Just as you always observe everyone else's. Perhaps it shouldn't be so. Maybe it shouldn't be a factor, but it is. If you are in poor condition, or overweight, or easily out of breath, you are less likely to be someone's inspiration. But that's good! Because you now have an opportunity. By taking up a new health program you can transform, physically, right before the eyes of your people. This is one of the most dramatic ways to be a role model for discipline and self-control ever. Steve recalls: I once lost 16 pounds by doing an extensive outdoor walking program and using the diet we introduced in Two Guys Read Moby Dick (Robert D. Reed Publishers, 2006). When I went back to do a workshop with a large team I'd worked with six months before, I was amazed at how many people came up and talked to me about the change in my appearance. I didn't think it mattered that much. But when I realized how pale and overweight I had been when they saw me six months ago compared to now, I got the picture. People care a lot whether you look healthy, vibrant, and alive. They associate poor physical condition with a kind of giving up inside...a depressed kind of caving in to last-ditch self-comforting. Studies show that if you appear strong and fit, you'll be better able to motivate others. Their subconscious response to you has more respect in it. On a subtle, psychological level, they admire your own commitment to excellence and discipline. (It's much harder to work hard for someone who does not take care of herself or himself.) Even changes in attire can be motivational (on a very subtle level, but it's true). As you take more care dressing well, it sends a message that life is good! It sends the message that this profession is important to you, so you want to look your best. You're a leader! So people notice when you upgrade your appearance in any way. Learning another language is a very challenging project, and we're not suggesting you take it on just to make an impression. But if it's something you were considering for professional or personal reasons, don't put it off. Because it's very inspiring to other people and often motivates them to expand their own skills in some category. Scott speaks fluent Spanish and Chinese, and the people at his law firm who get to see those skills demonstrated are inspired to use their own brains in new and powerful ways. Being a better speaker and meeting facilitator is open to anyone. Steve taught a class to graduate students at the University of Santa Monica in presentation skills for leaders. He said, "It's astonishing to me that even though many top level leaders in an organization speak to groups of people regularly, they very rarely enroll in a specific program to improve their skills." We've seen CEOs laugh off their own speaking skills and say, "I just try to be brief. Limit the damage! I'm not going to fool anyone. I'm not a pro. I'll just read my notes and be as brief as I can be. Thank goodness for PowerPoint." And what a missed opportunity that is. What if Churchill had taken that approach? There would have been no rallying of the British people to stand up to Hitler. Sometimes the very things leaders dismiss or try to get out of are what could turn the morale of the whole organization around. All human beings have the potential to speak well before a group. If you never dip into yours, you're not going to be much of an inspiration to anyone. We recommend that you, as a leader, take the Dale Carnegie classes (or some equivalent) in public presentation, and then let your people see the difference in your speaking skills. As you get better and better in front of a room of people, those same people will see the growth as it occurs. If speaking is already something you do well, you might choose listening as your next growth skill. Listening, compromise, positive reinforcement, compassionate relationshipbuilding, and all the other skills that build trust and understanding. There are books such as The Relationship Handbook (Pransky and Associates, 2001) by George Pransky and our own 50 Ways to Create Great Relationships (Career Press, 2000) that give a dramatic crash course in eliminating the sick ego in human communications. The University of Santa Monica's Spiritual Psychology program teaches leaders the deepest and most thoroughly generous listening skills on the planet. Many leaders we have worked with have enrolled in that program with dramatic turnarounds in team morale as a result. When you, as a true leader, learn to listen, everything opens up. You may choose customer relations as your next skill to improve. You can read Darby Checketts's Customer Astonishment (Robert D. Reed Publishers, 2006) and Positive Conflict (Career Pres, 2006) and take those books to heart. Your people will be astonished at how differently you treat customers and how much new business comes in as a result. They will remember you being rather brief and "professional" in demeanor with customers before, but now see you opening up to becoming a completely new you with whom customers love to brainstorm. When your people watch this, they get motivated like no other system or "trick" for motivating others will do. Why does it work so well? It's the hardest thing to do, and your people know it. A lot of older managers think it's cute or curmudgeonly to not want to learn any of the newer communication technologies. While the younger employees thrive on all kinds of "cool" new ways to communicate by phone, text, and videoconferencing, the stuck-in-the-past leader refuses to learn the new ways. A wonderful opportunity for personal growth is in the technical field. Every leader should subscribe to WIRED magazine and read it voraciously! You'll surprise everyone (in the most pleasant way) if you challenge yourself to stay current and continuously add new technical and Internet skills to your repertoire. When a new IT system comes in, you can be the first to learn it and embrace it. No one is really motivated by a same-ol', same-ol', stuck-in-the-past manager. If you think it's always a good thing to be falsely "consistent" as the same person you always were (stuck in an outdated rut), you are simply wrong. Most managers believe they don't have time to improve themselves by adding a new skill. They think they'd never have time to take a Dale Carnegie speaking class at night or fly into a weekend session at the University of Santa Monica because that's the time they reserve for stressing out over e-mails, or studying the sales reports, or being upset with their families. But it isn't a matter of time, it's a matter of commitment. It's a bold move to grow yourself in a new direction. That's why it's so motivating for others to watch you do it. When you pick your next category in which you improve yourself, make sure you really dive into it. Take it on with a passion. If you have a leadership coach (and we can recommend some good ones if you contact us at www.stevechandler.com), use that coach! Let him or her hold you accountable for dramatic change so that your people can see it and think "wow." Don't go through your life in leadership never tapping into that "wow" factor. It's always available to you. Not to mention the effect it will have on you yourself. As the great poet-philosopher William Butler Yeats said, "Happiness is neither this thing nor that...it is simply growth. We are happy when we are growing."

www.ingramcontent.com/pod-product-compliance
Ingram Content Group UK Ltd.
Pitfield, Milton Keynes, MK11 3LW, UK
UKHW021911190726
13853UKWH00002B/622